anne Barstow

Ministers of God,
Ministers of the People

Testimonies of Faith from Nicaragua

TEOFILO CABESTRERO

Translated from the Spanish by
Robert R. Barr

ORBIS BOOKS
Maryknoll, New York 10545

Zed Press
57 Caledonian Road
London N19DN

Second Printing, August 1984

The Catholic Foreign Mission Society of America (Maryknoll) recruits and trains people for overseas missionary service. Through Orbis Books Maryknoll aims to foster the international dialogue that is essential to mission. The books published, however, reflect the opinions of their authors and are not meant to represent the official position of the society.

Translated from the Spanish *Ministros de Dios, Ministros del Pueblo*, copyright © 1982 Teófilo Cabestrero

English translation © 1983 Orbis Books

Published jointly by Orbis Books, Maryknoll, NY 10545, and Zed Press, 57 Caledonian Road, London N1 9DN, U.K.

Manuscript editor: William E. Jerman

Library of Congress Cataloging in Publication Data

Cabestrero, Teófilo.
  Ministers of God, ministers of the people.

    1. Catholic Church—Nicaragua—Clergy—political activity.
2. Nicaragua—Politics and government—1979-   . I. Title.
BX1442.2.C32   1983   282'.7285   83-6306
ISBN 0-88344-335-X (pbk.)

British Library Cataloguing in Publication Data

Ministers of God, ministers of the people.
  1. Nicaragua—Politics and government
  2. Catholic Church—Clergy—Political activity
  I. Cabestrero, Teófilo
  354.7285   JL1609

  ISBN 0-86232-192-1
  ISBN 0-86232-193-X   Pbk

Contents

Preface

Teófilo Cabestrero is not exactly a household word in the First World. But we should become aware of him, for he is doing an important interpretive job acquainting us with "the other side of the news" from Central and South America. A Spanish priest-journalist, he had earlier given us a book-length interview with Bishop Pedro Casaldáliga of Brazil, entitled *Mystic of Liberation* (Orbis Books, 1981), the story of a brave bishop making his own "preferential option for the poor" in ways that have incurred the wrath of many elements within the Brazilian power structure—political, economic, and ecclesiastical—not to mention some not-so-hidden sources of Brazilian power: our own State Department, the CIA, the multinationals.

It is not without significance for our engagement with Teófilo Cabestrero's latest book of interviews, *Ministers of God, Ministers of the People,* that the earlier book is prefaced with a poem by Ernesto Cardenal, the subject of the initial interview in the pages that follow. In that poem we catch not only something of the spirit of Casaldáliga and Cardenal, but also some of the reasons for the involvement of the church in the Nicaraguan revolution as well.

Cardenal describes pictures of the day of the bishop's consecration,

> . . . with your mitre,
> which as we know is a palm-leaf hat,
> and your crozier, an oar from the Amazonia.

"The Military Police," Cardenal continues, addressing the bishop,

> . . . have told you
> that all the Church should worry about is "souls."
> But what about children starved by corporations?

iv

Scripture tells us that persons are to till the earth and possess it. But, Cardenal continues,

> How *shall they possess the earth* if the earth is owned by landlords?

Cardenal realizes, and knows that his bishop friend realizes, that

> the cross was
> for political criminals,
> not a cluster of rubies on a bishop's breast,

and that Pilate knew what was really going on in the revolution initiated by Jesus:

> Pilate stuck the sign up in four languages:
> SUBVERSIVE.
> > [Cabestrero, *Mystic of Liberation,* pp. ix–xiv]

The themes of the poem are appropriate not only in Brazil, but in Nicaragua as well—indeed in all of Central and South America, let alone the whole of what we call "the Third World," which is really the "two-thirds world" of the oppressed, victimized by the handfuls of those in their own countries who are overtly or covertly supported by the centers of industry and power in the United States and Europe.

The common themes are clear: the church must be engaged in struggle on the side of the poor; the authorities will try to limit the exercise of the church's concern to the "souls" of the poor and ignore the starvation of children; the impetus for the involvement of Christians is not simply political and economic analysis (though those may help), but is derived from the very nature of the Head of the church, who was executed as a political criminal, or, as Cardenal puts it even more bluntly, as a "subversive."

It is such concerns and motivations that have enflamed the hearts and lives of the three priests described in the following pages, Ernesto Cardenal, Fernando Cardenal, S.J., and Miguel d'Escoto, M.M. Each in his own way illumines the rich implications of the title, *Ministers of God, Ministers of the People.* None of them would suggest that they are engaging in other than a single ministry, for to be a minister of God is precisely to be a minister of the people. And for such convictions, these men have gotten caught in a double crossfire of criticism: on the one hand, from the church authorities in Rome, who consider it unseemly that priests should be so "political," and, on the other hand, from those who do not mind priests being "political" so long as their political tilt is to the right rather than the left. Let us consider each of these attacks in turn.

•

As far as the intramural conflict with their own hierarchy and the Vatican we can be brief, for Fr. Cabestrero has set out the sequence of events in his introduction. The three priests have been ordered to resign from their government posts as soon as possible, and in the interval while they are still in office they are to engage in no priestly duties, such as saying Mass, either in public or in private. (It is a sign of the deep religious motivations of the three that the latter stricture has been an especially painful cross for each of them to bear.) That the Vatican is displeased even with this arrangement was made dramatically clear to the world during the television coverage of the Pope's visit to Nicaragua, a visit he had earlier threatened to cancel if the three priests did not resign from public office. As John Paul II got off the airplane at Managua and greeted those gathered to meet him, he went down the line, shaking hands and offering his ring to be kissed. When he came to Fr. Ernesto Cardenal, however, the pope hastily withdrew his hand before it could be shaken or his ring kissed, and gestured with both hands in stern admonition, telling Fr. Cardenal in clear terms that he must straighten out his relation with the church.

I have learned by experience how fraught with possible misunderstandings are the attempts of non-Catholics to offer assessments of what is going on within Roman Catholicism, especially when the Vatican is involved. I will, however, risk restating an earlier observation, since it has been strengthened a hundredfold since reading the pages of this book. Whatever the canonical provisions for priests remaining out of public office, the Vatican can, when it wishes, waive the rule and make an exception (as it did during the first five terms Fr. Robert Drinan, S.J., served in the United States House of Representatives, only to withdraw the waiver summarily just a few weeks before the primary election for his sixth term). It can thus allow priests, under special circumstances, to participate directly in the process of government.

If ever there was a situation in which it would seem, to an outside observer, that the exception was appropriate, Nicaragua would appear to be that instance. Over the last century, a tremendous amount of Christian energy has been expended in a militant anti-communism, which almost inevitably translates itself into anti-socialism, and, in its final form, anti-anything-even-mildly-to-the-left-of-center. Those on the left have frequently returned the compliment by making the church, or the Christian faith itself, special targets for their polemics.

But in the case of Nicaragua, a new coalition government (surely tilting to the left, but still a coalition of wide political diversity) made special efforts to involve the three priests interviewed in this volume in the establishment of a new Nicaragua that would be the antithesis of everything the oppressive Somoza regime had represented. I believe one would search in vain for a parallel instance in which the government of a new regime, revolutionary in origin, recognized so clearly the importance of the contribution of the church.

To whatever degree there is the possibility, however imperfectly realized, of achieving "socialism with a human face" in Nicaragua, that possibility can only be enhanced and strengthened by the presence within the government of Frs. Cardenal and Fr. d'Escoto. Their loyalty to the church, to the teachings of Jesus, and to their priestly vows is beyond dispute, as the following pages will show. For them to leave public office rather than remain in it would create a vacuum at a time when persons of similar calibre and spiritual sensitivity are simply not yet available, and, to that extent, would contribute to the potential de-humanization of the new regime, thus helping to ensure self-fulfilling prophecies about the oppressive results of armed revolution by the left.

To the outsider, therefore, it would seem self-evident that the longer the three of them can participate in policy-making decisions within the Sandinista coalition, the more likelihood there is that the regime will move in directions creative and beneficial for all the people. That they can contribute greatly to the direction the revolution takes is patent. That Nicaragua needs them in their present positions seems equally apparent. One can only hope, therefore, that the ongoing frictions between the priests and Rome can be adjusted in such a way that the people of Nicaragua—and thereby all oppressed peoples who look to Nicaragua as a sign of hope—can continue to benefit from the presence in public office of men of such commitment and devotion to the cause of the poor and dispossessed.

•

We can introduce our second concern—the opprobrium heaped on these men for presuming that there is a connection between leftist politics and the Christian gospel—by an experience from a recent book by Fr. Henri Nouwen, an acknowledged expert on Roman Catholic spirituality, who recently spent six months living in Latin America trying to discover whether he had a vocation to live among the poor. Toward the end of his engaging account, *Gracias! A Latin American Journal* (Harper and Row, 1983), Fr. Nouwen describes reading the "Santa Fe Document," a paper written by Republicans in 1980 to propose a policy for the Reagan Administration in Latin America. The paper acknowledges that "in Latin America, the role of the Church is vital for the concept of political freedom"—which is true. It goes on, however, to say that "the Marxist-Leninist forces" have infiltrated "the religious community with ideas which are more Communist than Christian"—which is false. The foreign policy of the United States, the document asserts, must "start to confront . . . the theology of liberation as it is used in Latin America by the clergy of the 'liberation theology.' "

Fr. Nouwen confesses that he was greatly moved by these words, since "those who were setting the guidelines for the greatest power in the world consider theology a real threat." That such people should take theology so seriously seemed to Fr. Nouwen "among the greatest compliments to theology I have ever read." He continues, speaking of Gustavo Gutiérrez, author of *A Theology of Liberation* (Orbis Books, 1973):

> There is a little man in Peru, a man without any power, who lives in a *barrio* with poor people and who wrote a book. In this book he simply reclaimed the basic Christian truth that God became human to bring good news to the poor, new light to the blind, and liberty to the captives. Ten years later this book and the movement it started is considered a danger by the greatest power on earth. When I look at this little man, Gustavo, and think about the tall Ronald Reagan, I see David

standing before Goliath again with no more weapon than a
little stone, a stone called *A Theology of Liberation*.
                                   [Nouwen, *Gracias!,* pp. 174–175]

The imagery is helpful on a number of levels. It immediately
ties us in, for example, with Ernesto Cardenal, the first priest
interviewed in the present book, for it is this same Gustavo
Gutiérrez, the priest-activist working in Peru, who has said of
Ernesto Cardenal, the priest-poet working in Nicaragua, "In the
struggle in Latin America we need very much our poets." The
movement for a better society, in other words, does not involve
only political analysis, economic expertise, nor astute techniques
for change; it also involves a spirit welling up in the midst of a
people who have been exploited, and who must rally their forces
and spread their message not only by tracts and arguments, but
by songs, poems, paintings, posters, and concerns of the heart.
Ernesto Cardenal, as the interview reveals, is the purveyor of
such a spirit.

Not only, however, will the Davids of our day have such
resources at their disposal as *A Theology of Liberation* and the
poems of Ernesto Cardenal; they will also have an initial
commitment to literacy for all citizens, particularly the poor,
and an ongoing commitment to the youth of the land. When we
realize that the Latin American bishops at their Puebla meetings
in 1979 not only affirmed "a preferential option for the poor,"
but also (a fact less widely noticed) a preferential option for
youth, we see how important has been the ongoing contribution
in Nicaragua of Fr. Fernando Cardenal, S.J., who headed the
initial literacy program of the Sandinistas and has subsequently
been put in charge of his government's work with youth.

David's armaments begin to seem more substantial, and the
impression one receives after reading the interview with the
noted Jesuit educator is one of tremendous strength and undying
commitment.

This impression is further fortified by the responses of the
Maryknoll missioner, Fr. Miguel d'Escoto, who, like his
compatriots, not only sees no conflict between his priesthood
and his present role as Foreign Minister of the Sandinista
government, but an essential complementarity. (It was Fr.
d'Escoto who was named as the object of a projected United
States assassination attempt, in dispatches the Sandinistas
claimed to have intercepted; remembering earlier CIA attempts
on the life of Fidel Castro, the charge is at least consistent and

perhaps plausible.) Any questions that readers might initially bring to the motivations and concerns of a priest acting as foreign minister for a foreign power held by our own government to be inimicable to United States interests can be laid to rest by reading Fr. d'Escoto's reflections on the parable of the Good Samaritan (cf. pp. 111 and 114 below).

But we must not be deceived. David has not suddenly grown to the stature of Goliath, so that it is now an equal match. As the world understands power, these men have virtually none. As the world understands influence in high places, these men are noticeably lacking in the credentials to gain entrance. As the world counts the accoutrements of power—tanks, batallions, armies, military budgets—these men have no impressive statistics to present. But as the gospel understands power, in the sense of the spirit of people committed to a cause for which they are willing to die, and leadership in the sense of working with people to make decisions rather than imposing decisions upon them—in such terms, these men represent a power that will be invincible, no matter how "strong" the Goliath to the north may seem to be.

Goliath may win some temporary victories; indeed, these particular Davids may fall (a possibility each acknowledges to the interviewer), but there will be other Davids to take their places, others who may seem similarly weak and ill-equipped to do battle with a Pentagon-supplied Goliath, but upon whom that Goliath will ultimately be unable to impose his will.

Wherein lies the power of Goliaths, both ancient and modern? The power of Goliath does not lie in having a just cause but in exercising brute force. The power of Goliath does not lie in possession of the truth, but in the ability to tell a lie that sounds like the truth. The power of Goliath does not lie in a willingness to reason with the "enemy," but in a determination to destroy whatever "enemy" impedes Goliath from extending his will and power over the Davids of the world.

The present attempt of the government of the United States to destroy the government of the Sandinistas is a modern version of the David and Goliath story, and illustrates all the assertions of the previous paragraph. Our government supported a corrupt Somoza regime in Nicaragua for forty years, thus enabling, financing, and sponsoring the killing of tens of thousands of Nicaraguans; our government condoned the expropriation of peasant lands by the Somoza family to such a degree that if, after their fall from power, the family landholdings alone had been divided among the *campesinos* of Nicaragua, every family would have received five acres; our government supported and continues to support attempts to "destabilize" the Sandinista regime by withdrawing aid and urging others to do so; our government circulated a "White Paper" soon after Reagan came to office, claiming that a huge flow of arms was going from Russia to Cuba to Nicaragua to El Salvador, claims that the "White Paper" itself was unable to sustain in the face of even rudimentary scrutiny; our government has frequently announced that it will not negotiate with guerillas in El Salvador because it does not believe, in Secretary of State Shultz's words, in people "shooting their way into power," whereas in Nicaragua, where remnants of the Somoza regime are trying precisely to "shoot their way into power," our government is supporting them with arms, dollars, military training, technical assistance and a world-wide campaign to enlist support for them and bring about the fall of the Sandinista government.

When the El Salvador government murders fourteen thousand citizens in a single year, President Reagan certifies that the government is making substantial progress in "human rights" and should receive correspondingly substantial military aid; when Nicaragua engages in an admittedly controversial resettlement of Miskito Indians, our government issues photographs that it represents as Miskito Indians being burned by the Sandinistas, when the pictures are actually of the corpses of Somoza victims being burned by the International Red Cross for health reasons three years earlier.

The list of such deceptions, distortions and misrepresentations is almost endless. Goliath has made a decision that David shall be brought to his knees, and that power shall not be lodged with David's folk but with Goliath's camp followers. (For further documentation see the *National Catholic Reporter,* May 27, June 3, 1983.)

To those who feel that such charges and images are extravagant or even reckless, a simple test may be proposed: put on "hold" for the moment the stereotypes and impressions you receive about Nicaragua from the public press, and from such purveyors of that image to the press as Ronald Reagan, Casper Weinberger, and George Shultz. Read the following pages on their own terms, accepting for the moment that these three priests have been truly represented, and that they are sincere in what they say. Do the following images emerge: that these men are misguided individuals who have willfully "sold out" to

Marxism and traded the Lordship of Jesus Christ for the
leadership of Karl Marx? that the Sandinistas with whom they
work are nothing but a group of power-grabbing, irresponsible
terrorists intent only in bilking their own people for private
gain? that Ernesto Cardenal, Fernando Cardenal, and Miguel
d'Escoto are part of a grand design to extend atheistic
communism up the coast of Central America so that the United
States will totter and fall? that Marxist-Leninist theory has
prevailed over the concerns of these men to embody the
Christian gospel, so that terrorism and bloodshed are all that
exist in Nicaragua today? I suggest that those are not the images
that emerge.

The images that emerge are more like the following: here are
three men, deeply committed to God and therefore to God's
people, who have realized that in our day the injustices of the
world are so great that God must side with the victims of
injustice, and that those who love God must do the same; here
are three men whose devotion to the cause of Christ is the reason
for their political involvement with the poor; here are three men
who, on any human level, would prefer to be doing other things
but feel "called" to participate in the new government of their
land; here are three men who realize that their present activities
place them in personal jeopardy—jeopardy with the disap-
proving authorities of the church they love, and jeopardy with
political opponents who would like to destroy them; here are
three men who have said that they will not forsake the people
they are called to serve, whatever the inconvenience, danger, or
opprobrium; here are three men whose presence in the life of a
new government is a tribute to the trust in which they are held
even by those who do not share their faith; here are three men
who not only see no conflict between being "ministers of God"
and "ministers of the people," but could not even entertain
an understanding of priesthood that would put those two
descriptions in conflict.

Let them speak in their own name, in a response issued on
June 8, 1981, to an episcopal ultimatum insisting that they resign
from political office or face ecclesiastical sanctions:

> We believe in God the Father, Creator of the world and
>   human beings.
> We believe in Jesus Christ, the Son of God, our Brother and
>   our Savior.

We believe in the church, the visible Body of Christ, to which we belong.

We believe in justice, the basis of human community and communion.

We believe in love, the first and principal commandment of Jesus.

We believe in our priesthood, which is our vocation to serve our brothers and sisters.

We believe in our country, that great family to which we belong and to which we owe our being.

We believe in the Nicaraguan people's revolution, fashioned by the people in order to overthrow tyranny and sow justice and love.

We believe in the poor, who will be the ones to build a more just homeland, and who will help us to be saved ourselves [the full text of the document is printed below, p. 129].

•

The above pages have tried to be descriptive, although a certain authorial bias may not have escaped the reader. Let me therefore avoid any possible dissimulation and indicate clearly the perspective from which the above assessments are made, and the way in which the book helped to inform them.

We must avoid uncritical euphoria. The Sandinista government has not been without its mistakes. There have been some acts of censorship, there have been some deeds of repression. The government has not nearly delivered on all of its promises and it will be a long time in doing so. But it has also been the subject of relentless attack from the Reagan administration, not only verbally, but militarily and also economically (through attempts to manipulate the Nicaraguan economy toward what is euphemistically called "destabilization"), and by attempts, not very successful, to persuade other world governments to view Nicaragua as nothing but a new bastion of terror and oppression. Such an attitude is disheartening, since the Sandinistas' record of concern for *all* the people is incomparably better than that of its neighbors, El Salvador and Guatemala, which the same Reagan administration strongly supports.

The negative images of Nicaragua that our government is trying to maintain are challenged by the cumulative force of these interviews. So the lines are drawn more clearly than before. As a result, I close this book with gratitude that there are people in the world like Ernesto Cardenal, Fernando Cardenal, Miguel d'Escoto, and thousands of other Nicaraguans like them. And I close it with feelings of shame and anger that my own government is dedicated to trying to destroy everything for which they stand.

I am proud that the human race includes people of the stature of these three priests, and I pray that now and then a bit of their insight, character, and courage may rub off on me. And I am ashamed that the human race includes people who use fear-laden rhetoric, untruth, and military power, to extend their control over people who want no part of what they represent.

When I have to make a choice as to where the rightness and goodness and promise of the future are to be found, in this struggle between the perspectives of Ernesto Cardenal, Fernando Cardenal, and Miguel d'Escoto and the perspectives of Ronald Reagan, Casper Weinberger, and George Shultz, the decision is not a difficult one to discern, although it is a difficult one to affirm. I have to choose for the former and against the latter.

This is not a choice against my country, but it *is* a choice against those who claim to speak in the name of my country, and an assertion that I am not willing to let them speak for me. Albert Camus once wrote, "I should like to be able to love my country and still love justice." Let us hope that the Cardenals and the d'Escotos and all who work with them can empower us to work for a new situation in which we can again love our country and still love justice.

—*Robert McAfee Brown*

Introduction:
Priests in the
Nicaraguan Government

Law and Exception

I have been following very closely the phenomenon of priests in public office in the revolutionary government of Nicaragua for two and one half years now.

The Catholic Church forbids its priests and religious to hold political office or engage in public activity on behalf of a political party, in order the better to safeguard the exercise of their priestly office and to safeguard their witness of Christian love. Pope John Paul II has mentioned this repeatedly in discourses to priests and religious the world over.

But the church also grants exceptions to this law, in consideration of exceptional situations—emergencies. Cardinal Eduardo Pironio, in a communication issuing from the Sacred Congregation of Religious in Rome and directed to the religious of the entire world, wrote (August 1980):

> Active political participation must be considered an exception, a "supplementary ministry," and must be evaluated according to special criteria. When extraordinary circumstances require, each such case must be examined in particular, in order to draw (with the approval of those responsible for the local church and the religious institutes) conclusions that may redound to the good of the ecclesial and civil community.

1

Indeed the church has a long tradition of humane service, or "supplementary ministry," not directly essential to its Christian ministry as such, but nevertheless consonant with its global message of love and integral liberation. Understandably, this "supplementary ministry" is a common thing for priests and religious ministering to peoples of the Third World. It often provides the only means of accomplishing the objective of the general law cited above: the witness of Christian love, the performance of the ministry of the salvific love of God our Father for all women and men. To refuse to perform these supplementary ministries would be to refuse love and to fail to accomplish one's ecclesial mission considered in its globality.

The history of the church—and the life story of many a priest, religious, and missionary—is replete with these supplementary ministries. These "exceptions," these services that "supply" for a lack, are not grudging concessions, to be withdrawn as soon as possible. There have been times in the history of certain peoples when these ministries have constituted the only way, or at least the best way, for the church to carry out its mission from God to humanity. They are altogether traditional in the history of the church.

Falling into the category of "exceptions to the law," then, supplementary ministries are at the mercy of human discernment. Hence they call for clarification and analysis, in each emergency situation and each need, in order to provide the basis for a diagnosis of the degree of urgency of a prospective exception. An ongoing, honest, serene, and lucid dialogue is an indispensable tool in the process of this clarification. This all-important dialogue must have the active participation of all parties directly involved: the hierarchy of the church, with its advisors and its communities; the priests or religious who would be the grantees of these exceptions, along with their superiors; the representatives of the competent civil authority who have called for the services of these priests or religious.

Nicaragua, 1979–81

On July 19, 1979, the revolution was victorious in Nicaragua. The new government of national reconstruction called for the active involvement of certain priests and religious in the governmental process. The situation was an emergency one, resulting from the excesses of the Somoza regime and from the bloody war of liberation that had overthrown that regime. The disproportion between the immense tasks to be performed and the scarcity of available resources created an "exceptional situation" and required the "supplementary services" of certain priests and religious.

The new government first appointed two priests to cabinet posts. Father Miguel d'Escoto, a Maryknoll missionary, became foreign minister. The poet Ernesto Cardenal, a monk of Solentiname, was named minister of culture.

In August of the same year (1979), Jesuit Father Fernando Cardenal was appointed national coordinator of the National Crusade for Literacy. The campaign was six months in preparation (from October 1979 to March 1980) and five months in execution (from March 23 to August 23, 1980) and availed itself of the technical services of priests, as well as men and women religious.

As the literacy crusade neared its close, Father Fernando was named to the post of national vice-coordinator of the Sandinista Youth Movement (July 19, 1980).

In August 1980, Father Edgar Parrales, a pastor in Managua, who had already been serving in the area of social welfare in the government, was appointed minister of social welfare. Later, this ministry was fused with the Institute of Social Security, and a Catholic layman, Reinaldo Antonio Tefel, became minister. Father Parrales went to the United States to represent the government of Nicaragua in the Organization of American States.

A number of priests and religious provide technical and support services in both government and popular organizations.

Along other lines, Jesuit Father Alvaro Argüello has been the delegate of the Nicaraguan Clergy Association (ACLEN) to the Council of State since 1980.

In September 1980, Fathers Miguel d'Escoto, Fernando Cardenal, and Ernesto Cardenal were elected to the Sandinista Assembly.

Chronology of a Crisis

All through 1980 and 1981, the world watched an exchange of letters and other documents between the Nicaraguan bishops and the priests in government positions. Here are some of the milestones in the evolution of that correspondence.

1) On May 13, 1980, feast of Our Lady of Fatima, with the literacy crusade in full swing, the bishops expounded on the proper functions of hierarchy, clergy, and laity respectively, declared the "exception" terminated, and asked that the supplementary ministries cease. "We consider," they wrote, "that, inasmuch as the circumstances constituting the exception now no longer obtain, Christian lay persons can just as efficiently discharge the public duties now being performed by certain priests."

2) On May 20, ten priests and religious serving in the government signed a letter expressing their readiness, as servants of the church, to engage in a dialogue with the bishops: "Our loyalty to the church and our loyalty to the poor cannot be in contradiction," they said.

3) On October 17, in response to the Official Declaration of the National Leadership of the FSLN on Religion, the bishops referred to the assignment of priests to government positions as "patronage and flattery," calculated to divide the church by utilizing these priests as "naive tools" for political ends.

4) On March 23, 1981, certain statements by Father Edgar Parrales in the Mexican periodical *Proceso,* including critical questions for the bishops, heightened the tension.

5) On June 1, 1981, the bishops issued an ultimatum to Nicaraguan priests in the government: either they resign from office as soon as practicable, or sanctions would be imposed. The bishops expressed their regret that their earlier suggestions and communications had not led the "ecclesiastical persons concerned" to give up their offices. Finally, after citing "pastoral and theological considerations," church "laws," and certain Catholic teachings, they wrote:

In conclusion, we wish to state that, having brought everything concerning this matter to the attention of the Holy

See, and having been assured of its total support and authorization to proceed in accordance with our grave responsibility as pastors:

a) We emphatically reaffirm what we stated in our Pastoral Message of May 13, 1980.

b) We declare that, if the priests who occupy public positions and exercise party functions do not resign these responsibilities as soon as possible, and devote all their activity to their specifically priestly ministry, we would have to consider them to be in a position of open rebellion and formal disobedience to legitimate ecclesiastical authority, and thus subject to penalties provided by the laws of the church.

6) On June 8, 1981, in a "first response" to the episcopal ultimatum, four of the priests to whom it had been addressed—Fathers Miguel d'Escoto, Ernesto Cardenal, Edgar Parrales, and Fernando Cardenal—made a public profession of their Christian faith and hope and reaffirmed their commitment both of fidelity to their priestly vocation and of obedience to the will of God in the service of the people.

7) On June 30, after a visit to Rome by a government delegation and a dialogue with the Vatican secretary of state, Cardinal Agostino Casaroli, as well as a similar visit to Rome by the president and secretary of the Bishops' Conference, the Nicaraguan bishops issued a new communiqué to the priests in question:

Keeping ever in view the institutional norms of the church, the policy of the Holy See, and our particular circumstances, we have determined to address you in the following tenor:

a) Faithful to our church and to our pastoral mission, we emphatically reaffirm what we stated in our documents of May 13, 1980, and June 1, 1981.

b) Although several conversations have already been held on this matter, without our having received any direct and definitive response from you, yet in a spirit of brotherhood, and for the greater good of all, we are disposed to receive you on either the 13th or the 15th of July 1981, at your good pleasure.

c) The object of this new conversation would be to clarify a situation that lends itself to confusion and tendentious interpretations.

8) On July 7, 1981, the four priests replied:

Both in person and in personal letters, especially in our letters of May 20 and December 25, 1980, we have manifested our desire to be granted the opportunity to enter upon a sincere dialogue, a dialogue in depth, in the light of the gospel, with Your Excellencies. Your communiqué of June 30 fills us with hope; it gives us to believe we have not hoped in vain.

We want to engage in dialogue with the bishops. We seek a dialogue that will be as rich and useful as it can possibly be. Therefore we believe that it is necessary that all of us share in this dialogue, together with all the members of the Bishops' Conference.

The four priests proposed July 13 as the date for the meeting.

9) On July 15, at the conclusion of the meeting between the bishops and the four priests, with the participation of the papal nuncio to Managua, Archbishop Andrea Cordero Lanza di Montezémolo, the bishops issued a closing communiqué. Their declaration opened with a lengthy statement of doctrinal "principles" concerning priests and the priestly mission; then it went on to refer to the dialogue that had been held with the four priests:

Faced with the choice of continuing in the discharge of their governmental functions or of devoting themselves to the service of their proper tasks in the priestly ministry, they, after having set forth their reasons, expressed their conviction that their personal presence in the government continued to be necessary. Seeking, nevertheless, to remain faithful to the norms and principles of the church, they proposed a plan to provide for the exceptional situation, in order to be able to continue in their present tasks, on the following basis:

a) They would maintain, in all things, their identity of faith in communion with the hierarchy.

b) They recognized that what is prejudicial to the church is prejudicial to the people, in its demands for and need of integral liberation and development.

c) They requested that, rather than renounce their priestly vocation, they be granted a state of temporary exception, under the following conditions:

- That, so long as they exercise public duties, or party functions, they abstain from all exercise of the priestly ministry, whether public or private, at home or abroad.
- That they make no attempt to utilize or invoke their priesthood in order to justify positions proceeding from their civil incumbencies or their political options.
- That, in order to secure their ecclesial communion, they maintain contact with the ecclesiastical hierarchy.

The bishops concluded with a statement of "temporary toleration" of this situation of exception, adding that they "reiterated, with absolute insistence," their directive that priests in government "return as soon as possible to the exercise of their priestly ministry."

A Sixteen-Month Truce

This last episcopal communiqué ended the crisis of the "padres in the government," which had so exercised both Christian and non-Christian sectors, revolutionaries and nonrevolutionaries. There had been meetings, declarations, documents, letters, and the like, in every quarter. Now things were clear, and the crisis seemed resolved.

Nicaraguans—a revolutionary Christian people—wanted these priests to continue in their public charge. They saw no conflict with their being ministers of God. They did not judge the "exception" to have terminated. On the contrary, it was all the more pressing, for the emergency had become more grave.

All was calm again. Public opinion, as expressed in the media, no longer even alluded to the old problem. For two years, in so-called independent circles, frequent campaigns of harsh castigation had been conducted against priests in the government. Now revolutionary sectors overflowed with solidarity and support for these same priests.

But there was nothing in the media—until, in November 1982,

the Managua daily, *La Prensa,* reported that Archbishop
Obando y Bravo had made the following statement to the
students of the minor seminary in Managua, in his exhortation
on the occasion of the closing of the scholastic year: "May the
seminarians we form here be deeply devoted to the Blessed
Virgin and faithful to God, and not suddenly turn out to be the
servants of an impoverished ideology." And—again, according
to *La Prensa*—he cried out how "sad it would be if, after
all the efforts the seminary had made in their training for the
priesthood, they would become great ministers, yes, but not
great priests."

Some days later, on December 3, 1982, the *New York Times*
ran a front-page story, under the by-line of Marlisa Simons,
which neither the Vatican nor the government of Nicaragua
confirmed or denied. Said the *Times:*

> Pope John Paul II has demanded that Roman Catholic priests
> resign from positions they hold in the Nicaraguan
> Government as a condition for his visiting Nicaragua early
> next year, Roman Catholic Church officials here said.
>
> The Pope's ultimatum was personally delivered to the
> coordinator of the Nicaraguan junta, Daniel Ortega
> Saavedra, in late October by the Papal Nuncio here
> [Managua], Msgr. Andres Cordero Lanza di Montezemolo,
> the officials said. . . .
>
> Attention has focused on five priests in highly visible
> positions: the Rev. Miguel d'Escoto Brockmann, who is
> Foreign Minister; the Rev. Ernesto Cardenal, the Minister of
> Culture; the Rev. Edgar Parrales, now Nicaragua's
> Ambassador to the Organization of American States; the
> Rev. Fernando Cardenal, a leader of the official Sandinist
> Youth movement; and the Rev. Alvaro Argüello Hurtado,
> who represents the clergy on the Council of State.

The Unknown Factor

In principle, the relationship between law and exception is
perfectly clear to me. I have always understood that when a
priest is exercising a "supplementary ministry," as the

exceptional need gradually disappears and the supplementary ministry loses its urgency—because others can now be found who can fill the need more meaningfully—that priest ought to give it up. He should once more serve the people and its cause in his specifically priestly capacity and mission, according to his own charism.

But I would not venture to determine on my own authority—at my own risk, as it were—how long the exception or exceptional need continues—how long this supplementary ministry maintains its appropriateness, and when it loses that appropriateness. For this, a concrete analysis of the situation is indispensable. Dialogue is irreplaceable. This is especially the case in Nicaragua, where the circumstances are so new and unusual.

In all their communiqués and correspondence, the bishops and priests spoke of the need for dialogue. But they never managed to achieve it. They never managed to engage in really clear, positive, trustful dialogue, a dialogue of mutual assistance and support, in which all would contribute their insights and their energies in a community of quest, and share both the fruits and limits of that quest. Never. The required conditions were not present. There was not that climate of trust and confidence, that climate of mutual approach and appreciation, needed for such a dialogue.

I used to watch these "padres in government" at some of their meetings. And I would ask myself, What are they thinking and feeling? What is going on inside them? What is their interior experience in all this—their faith, their pain, their hope, their fears, their temptations? They have, of course, their own personal stories, their sensitivities, their reasoning, their wounds, their emotions, their desires, their hopes.

And I said to myself that there must be, in each of them, a given quantity of generosity, of faith, of sin perhaps, and conversion, too. And these quantities must be different from mine, because their experience is different from mine. Theirs is more of a "front-line experience." In the personal experience of each one of them, an experience that can never be repeated or duplicated, there must be something of the gospel, I thought, something of the Spirit of God—a little or a lot—but surely something. In each of them. Was not God perhaps trying to tell all of us something through them? Would the church not lose a new trove of spiritual wealth if it did not consider, lovingly, the personal witness and experience of each of them?

It seemed to me that this was an essential factor, of which account would have to be taken in any dialogue worth the having. But the circumstances, the atmosphere, the tension, the nervousness—the failure to have a real dialogue—had brought it about that precisely this factor was the unknown one. Were the church and the world to lose what these individuals harbored of God's newness—their share of the surprises God has in store for each of us in our singular, unique personal experience? And I decided to seek out their witness one day, their experience of faith on the front line, and share it with all.

That day has come. I have obtained the personal testimony of three of them. I should like to take this occasion to express to them my sincere and deep gratitude. And I offer this testimony, with all my heart, to the world, in the conviction that, wherever we have a sincere witness to love, faith, service, and sacrifice, there we have a revelation—a revelation of God, a revelation of the gospel, a revelation of truth, life, and meaning. To be sure, their witness has its limits, too—its peculiarities, its particularities of personal vision that will be open to dispute. The reader will see this. Nevertheless, faith, the gospel, and Christ himself are communicated in their witness.

I offer this testimony with the eager, loving desire that the church not lose, either for itself or for the world, anything it can have of gospel, grace, and the Spirit in the experience and witness of each and every one of its sons and daughters who struggle, who battle, who risk—not out of caprice, or selfishness, or wickedness, but with faith and love.

I find myself strengthened and encouraged in this sentiment by something Cardinal Pironio said in the letter from which I have already quoted:

> The situation of religious in Central America merits special attention. I think that a judgment passed on them from abroad would be superficial. In particular, it would be unjust

to condemn attitudes that, however questionable or even wrong, are intended as a response of faith to Jesus Christ, to the church, and to the concrete historical situation of the people. There is a great deal of evangelical sacrifice in all of this. And much prayer. This is a providential moment for Latin America.

*"Being minister of culture is a cross for me.
I'm not a politician. I'm a revolutionary,
I'm a monk, I'm a poet."*

Ernesto Cardenal,
Minister of Culture

Ernesto Cardenal was born in Granada, Nicaragua, January 20, 1925. He was already writing verse at the age of seven. He received his primary and secondary education from the Jesuits of his home city (1935 to 1942).

In 1942 he went to Mexico City, to study at the National Autonomous University. He published a number of poems, in Mexican periodicals, and in 1947 received his licentiate in letters (master's degree). That same year he went to the United States, to study American literature at Columbia University, New York City (1948 and 1949).

After some travels in Europe (France, Italy, Spain, and Switzerland), Cardenal returned to Nicaragua, in 1950, where he began to write his historical poems and translate North American poetry. His short love poems reflect his emotional relationships of the period. His militant opposition to the dictatorship of General Somoza inspired his political epigrams. In 1954 he took part in the armed movement known as the April Rebellion, which planned an assault on the presidential palace. The plan was betrayed, and some of Cardenal's friends died as a result.

In 1956, Ernesto experienced a religious conversion. Suddenly the direction of his life changed. He decided to become a monk, and at the age of thirty-two, in 1957, entered the Trappist monastery of Our Lady of Gethsemani, in Kentucky. Thomas Merton was his novice master and counselor; they became friends.

Ernesto left the Trappists in 1959, for reasons of health, and entered the Benedictine monastery of Cuernavaca, Mexico.

13

There he studied for two years, writing a number of poems on
the Trappist life, a book of meditations, *Vida en el amor* ("life
in love"), and a long historical poem entitled "El estrecho
dudoso" ("predicament and doubt").

From 1961 to 1965, Cardenal studied for the priesthood in a
seminary in Colombia. He published his *Salmos* ("psalms") and
his *Oración por Marilyn Monroe* ("prayer for Marilyn
Monroe") during this period. He also began his poems on the
Amerindians, which were to appear under the title *Homenaje a
los indios americanos* ("homage to the American Indians").
In 1965, at the age of forty, Ernesto was ordained a priest in
Managua. He immediately went to visit Thomas Merton again,
to finalize plans for the foundation of a contemplative
community in Nicaragua. Then, on February 13, 1966, Father
Ernesto, with William Agudelo and Carlos Alberto, founded the
community of Solentiname, on the chain of islands of that name
in Lake Nicaragua.

In 1970 he visited Cuba. His perception of the Cuban
revolution is recorded in his book *En Cuba* ("in Cuba"). From
that time onward, it is the revolution that governs his travels (to
Peru, Chile, and New York), his long poems, *Viaje a Nueva
York* ("journey to New York"), *Canto nacional* ("national
hymn"), *Oráculo sobre Managua* ("oracle on Managua"), and
his Christian reflection on the Solentiname community, *El
Evangelio en Solentiname* (English translation, *The Gospel in
Solentiname*, 4 vols.).

Ernesto Cardenal represented the *Frente Sandinista de
Liberación Nacional* (FSLN, Sandinista National Liberation
Front) before the Russell Tribunal, which met in Rome in 1976
to pass judgment on violations of human rights in Latin
America. The youth of the Solentiname community joined the
FSLN. Some of them took part in the assault on the San Carlos
Barracks in 1977. Somoza's National Guard destroyed
Solentiname, after Cardenal's escape from Nicaragua, and
thereafter he devoted himself to support missions for the FSLN
in various countries of the world.

Once the insurrection was victorious, in July 1979, a new
Nicaraguan government was set up. Ernesto Cardenal was

named minister of culture, the office he still holds at the time of this writing (December 1982).

Ernesto Cardenal's poetical work is recognized as one of the most important contributions to Latin American literature in this century.

•

The old Somoza mansion, where the dictator had lived, is on an immense estate not far from his bunker near the center of Managua. Today it houses the ministry of culture.

I went to the minister's office four times for interviews with him, for a total of seven hours of conversation. On one of these visits, in his outer office, I had the occasion to greet Uruguayan author Eduardo Galeano. Another time, again in the outer office, the Nicaraguan poet Julio Valle Castillo read me a poem of his, addressed to Laureano Mairena, in Solentiname. Three days before, Captain Mairena had been struck down by the Falk, a band of counterrevolutionaries, in the hills of Yumpali, near the Honduran border to the north. Then someone came in and began talking with Valle Castillo, saying, at one point, "Tell the poet that!" He was referring, of course, to Ernesto Cardenal, the minister of culture (whom I noticed the secretary always called "Father").

To get to this office, you take a delightful walk, from where city bus 119 brings you, away from the noise of the city, along the road that Somoza built to his mansion. You pass beneath a huge *chilamate* tree—a gigantic tree with a monstrous trunk and very fine leaves. You pass the old checkpoint of Somoza's National Guard. Nothing is checked there now; there is no guard. Access is open and free. You go up the lane of lemon trees—short little trees with their snowflake blossoms the color of cinnamon—and over the lemon trees you can make out Lake Managua, the mountains that bathe there, and Momotombo Volcano. Finally, you come into the dark grove of some more *chilamate* trees, with their big, shiny leaves, and just beyond you spy the building that houses the ministry of culture, behind the high, inaccessible walls that hid the dictator's private hours, and that now provide a home for the work of the popularization of culture in the new Nicaragua.

The building retains the lordliness and elegance of its modern colonial style. There on the patios are the old tree trunks standing between the blind walls and the great windows. It is said that a huge *chilamate*, which had reigned over the garden, was mysteriously uprooted one night, and was found lying on its side in the dawn light, two days before Somoza was killed in a bazooka attack in Asunción, Paraguay.

The ground floor of the ministry is a honeycomb of offices. Revolution is on every wall, in posters, in paintings, in murals. A wooden staircase leads to the antechamber of the minister's office on the second floor.

I always found Ernesto dressed the same: same blue jeans, same white cotton shirt (the Nicaraguan peasant's shirt), same black beret—and those glasses of his, as white, and as much he, as his big head of hair and his beard. He dressed the way he had in Solentiname.

And so there we sat, face to face, across his enormous, light-colored wooden table. When I was speaking, asking the questions, Ernesto looked at me with an intense regard that betrayed no emotion. When he answered, he lowered his head a bit, and his beard and hair seemed to branch out and fuse with his white cotton shirt. He would lower his eyelids until his eyes were nearly closed, or else he would stare at the tabletop. He spoke slowly, working his sentences, measuring his words, making an effort to modulate his dark, grave voice. From time to time he would light up a cigarette, smoke, and be silent. I did not interrupt then. Finally he would continue—working, constructing. He told me of his life, his work, his reasoning—and I received an elocution lesson into the bargain.

> **"Christ has put me in charge
> of spreading culture."**

"Since July 19, 1979," I said to Ernesto, "the day the Sandinista popular revolution triumphed, you've been Nicaragua's minister of culture. Nearly four years have passed—very difficult years, years filled with conflict. And

*you're a poet, you've been a monk, and you're a priest. There
are many who do not understand this. It seems strange to
them—contradictory—that you should hold this office. You
have your reasons, and your personal experience, and I think
we'll have to know what these are if we're not to judge you
blindly. What is your personal experience, Ernesto? How do you
perform the duties of minister of culture in the revolution
without contradicting your priestly office?"*

"For us, Ernesto replied, the revolution is love. And by love
we mean love of neighbor—concern for adequate nourishment
for everybody, improvement in the quality of life for the whole
population, making sure everyone has decent housing, making
sure there are medical services for everybody, education and
culture for everybody, recreation, care of the elderly, child
care—in other words, a society of brothers and sisters.

"I wrote a poem about how busy we were those first days
after victory, carrying out those tasks. The name of the poem is
'Busy.' I describe how we were busy with so many things—land
distribution, digging up the bodies of the murdered, rebuilding
bombed hospitals, creating a new police force, getting drinking
water to so many places, electrification, creating new
marketplaces, new parks, keeping track of the price of staple
grains, repairing roads, working on the Campaign for Literacy
that would teach a million Nicaraguans to read, planning
education, clearing away debris, working the fields. . . . And
these tasks are the same ones we keep doing today—only, you
see, in those first days we did them with more urgency, with
feverish urgency, because everything had to be done at once.

"I have a poem in which I describe a cabinet meeting. The
name of the poem is simply 'Cabinet Meeting.' It's about how
all the ministers have been called together for a very important
reason, but we don't know what the reason is. And the reason
turns out to be the creation of a national emergency committee
for the problem of the aëdes mosquito—an extremely serious
problem for children, and dangerous for the elderly, because
this mosquito carries dengue. So there's an epidemic to be
avoided. And after I describe this cabinet meeting in some
detail, I end up by saying that I look at the serious faces around

the big table where all the ministers are gathered, and I think: 'Strange—a cabinet meeting for love of neighbor.'

"For me, the revolution is what Camilo Torres called it: 'efficacious charity,' charity in action. He called it efficacious because it's not individual charity, it's on the national level, and this is the only way charity can be effective in society. And Camilo also said that the revolution is a Christian and a priestly task, and that's what it is for me.

"I have said many times that the governmental program of the Sandinista front is to feed the hungry, clothe the naked, teach the ignorant—to give everything to those who have nothing.

"Before I ever became minister of culture, before victory, I knew that ministry meant service, and minister meant servant. That goes for government ministry and ministers just as much as for priestly ministry and ministers. I had this explained to me very well in a cabinet meeting in Belize. The prime minister there is deeply Christian, a real Catholic. He and one of his ministers up there, the minister of education and health, told me how they had a retreat every month, to examine their consciences and see where they had failed the people, where they hadn't been good servants of the people. And they told me that minister of government means the same thing as minister of religion. It means a servant.

"Now I happen to have this other ministry too, besides the priestly ministry. I have the job of promoting everything cultural in the country. I have the ministry of music, of poetry, of painting, of crafts, of theater, of folklore and tradition, of scholarly research of our whole national heritage—museums, libraries, magazines, cultural institutions, films, recreation, all those things. I have the ideological ministry. And it's interesting that this ideological ministry, which means so much to the revolution, should have been entrusted to a priest—just as the ministry of foreign affairs, which is the most important ministry in any country, but especially in a revolutionary one, has been entrusted to a priest. And the Campaign for Literacy, which is not just for literacy, but is also a political and ideological campaign, was also entrusted to a priest, my brother Fernando. And now he's been put in charge of our young people's training in the Sandinista Youth Movement. And in economic planning, where the economic future of our country is being planned, there's another priest. And the ministry of education has been given to a militant Christian lay person. The ministry of housing and the social welfare ministry have also gone to militant Christian lay persons. All this indicates the confidence the revolution has in Christians and priests.

"As far as culture is concerned, there has been a powerful cultural rebirth since the victory of the revolution. Along with material goods, spiritual goods have priority too. We don't conceive of material welfare without spiritual welfare. And as Christ placed his Apostles in charge of distributing the loaves and fishes, I feel he's placed me in charge of spreading culture."

> *"My vocation is more monastic than priestly. What I did in Solentiname, I now do on a larger scale."*

"This means sacrifices for me, certainly," Ernesto continued. "The biggest one is the renunciation of my literary work. There is almost no time left for writing. I have so little time for this, and so many things to write, and I feel I'm in the last stage of my maturity as a writer. This is not the first time I've made this sacrifice. When I entered the Trappists I was told I couldn't write, and I willingly accepted it. I accept it willingly now, too, because the reason I don't write is that I'm getting others to write poetry and make music and have theater and singing and dance.

"And I like it very much when I see the poems of the new poets, when I see the paintings of new artists, when I see the great progress we are making in the crafts, in the popular arts—when I see that the people not only 'gets' culture, it participates in culture, it creates its own culture. I consider all this priestly and monastic—especially monastic.

"I should like to clarify something for you. My personal vocation has not been precisely priestly, but monastic. The life of a monk has always been one of farm work and cultural work.

And in Solentiname, where I spent twelve years trying to live the monastic life, I devoted myself to promoting agriculture among the *campesinos* of the countryside, as much as we could, by teaching them new techniques, raising better seed grain for them, starting cooperatives, and so on. And we encouraged painting, by starting a school of primitive painting in Solentiname, which acquired quite a reputation in many places in the world—in many countries of Latin America, in New York, Paris, Germany, Switzerland, and so on. And we encouraged crafts among the country people; their works have been exported and have been very well received in many places. And we got them to write good poetry, which has been published in Nicaragua, and in other countries in various languages.

"Now, if all this looks to be in keeping with my priestly and monastic state, then what I have to do now as minister of culture is simply to do all this on a large scale, all over Nicaragua, and not just for the thousand inhabitants of the Solentiname islands."

> *"I offer to God all the trips and official parties I don't like."*

"It's the same with my trips abroad. I have to take a lot of trips, not so much as minister of culture, but mainly for the revolution. These trips are a great sacrifice for me. When I was in Solentiname, where I lived a life of isolation, solitude, and retreat for twelve years, many times I would see, in magazines, ads for travel agencies, directed at tourists. And I would sometimes feel the longing to leave that isolation and travel to exotic places. But alas, I considered that it was my lot to remain where I was. And now suddenly this has changed, and I have to take such long trips that I get the idea that this must be some kind of humorous punishment by God, as if he said, 'Fine, you want to travel? So travel.'

"Ever since about two years before the victory of the revolution, much of my life has been lived on airplanes. I have traveled to all the countries of Latin America I could without being killed, to the United States, Canada, Europe, all Western

Europe—that is, Spain, Portugal, Italy, France, Belgium, the
Netherlands, Switzerland, Finland, Luxembourg—I don't know
if I've skipped any—and several of the socialist countries of
Europe. And Lybia, Beirut several times, Syria, Iraq, Iran.

"I remember what I was told about Father Lombardi, who
chased all over the world with those famous sermons. They said
he'd made a vow never to be a tourist, in any country, so as not
to take advantage of those trips for any personal enjoyment.
They were to be just for evangelization. I never made that vow,
but I've kept it, in practice, all the same. Once on my way
through Greece I spent half an hour at the Acropolis. In Iraq I
took time to see the ruins of Babylon. But these were exceptions.
Nearly always, I pass through countries without getting to know
them. I get only the hard part of a trip.

"The real trials for me are the social obligations of
officialdom, especially official diplomatic receptions. Not long
ago I wrote a poem in which I talk about going to a diplomatic
reception—of course I won't name the embassy—and how I saw
a cat on my way there, in the gutter, and how much I wanted to
get out and stay there and watch the cat, to write something
about it, and not go where I was going. But as I was thinking
this, suddenly there I was walking into the brightly lighted
embassy and greeting the ambassador. Another time, at a dinner
a minister was having for me—I musn't say where this one was,
either—it suddenly became clear to me what some of the mystics
meant by the 'sweetness of the cross,' the satisfaction one
sometimes finds in suffering. I was really suffering there, but I
found sweetness in the suffering. And don't think it was the
dinner or the music or the folk dancing!

"My novice master in the Trappists, Thomas Merton, used to
tell us that later on in the monastic life there would be moments
of unbearable dryness, aridity. Our novitiate life was very
cheerful and happy. But he warned us what the future held in
store. He used to say that sometimes when a monk gets up in the
morning to go from the dormitory to the choir, he has to make a
superhuman effort to traverse the little stretch of corridor from
the dormitory to the choir. Every step costs, and the monk has
to overcome himself just to get to choir! This is what happens to
me sometimes when I'm going to a reception, or to one of those

formal dinners. I have to make an enormous effort to put one foot in front of the other, and I have a great temptation not to go. But I have to go; it's an obligation. We've been told that it's part of the work of our office, and we understand that it's not a matter of an amusement that one may happen to like or not like.

"I've also used the example of Che Guevara, which I heard about in Cuba. I was told that Che always went to official receptions out of a pure sense of duty. Everybody knows that the last thing Che could have been accused of was enjoying himself at receptions. He would severely upbraid ministers who failed to attend. He would tell them that they were supposed to do this for the people, and that they were not sacrificing themselves for the people if they failed to attend. So, fine, I decided I would always go—but what I could do would be to go there, stay a little while, and then leave. So I asked the Cubans whether Che just showed up and left like that. And they told me that if the reception was from eight to ten, Che would be there at eight, on the dot, and leave at ten.

"Fine, so I go, and I always offer it up to God. And I think of the people, too—I keep thinking, 'We're doing this for the people.'

"My life as a government minister is very hard. It and the Trappist noviceship are the hardest things I have ever had to do in my life. The hardest thing for me in the Trappists was the physical work in the fields, peasant work; the Trappists are a rural-based, nonliterary order. The hardest thing for me as a minister is in the line of the spiritual—not being able to spend my time the way I want, having to go to meetings, and doing things I have to make a great act of the will to put up with, especially social functions. But I consider that I'm doing the will of God.

"The will of God has been expressed in my life in various ways. First it led me to the silence of a Trappist monastery. Then it led me to the isolation of the Solentiname islands. Then it led me to other countries, to do a great variety of things for the Sandinista Front—so many trips, all over the world. And now it's led me to be minister of culture. But I figure that there is just one line in my life that God's been leading me along, first in one way and then in another. I figure that all this has been the will of God. This gives me a great deal of peace—total peace.''

> *"There's a lot of loneliness in my life, and it will end only when I die."*

"I'm at peace, in spite of the frustrations of this assignment. Naturally, there are frustrations in any job—things that don't work out for you, no matter whose fault it is, your friends' or your enemies'. What I do is not worry about these things, not make anything out of them, but keep at peace within myself.

"I often recall an anecdote I heard about John XXIII, how when he had problems he was very worried about he would say to himself, 'John, John, aren't you taking yourself too seriously?' So this is what I say to myself—that I'm taking myself too seriously, and that it is not so terrible if a few things don't come out so well, or if *I* don't come off well. And so my frustrations don't bother me.

"And death—the ultimate frustration—I'm not afraid of it. Once I turned myself over to God, and renounced all things, from that moment on I have nothing to lose.

"Yes, my life is very much a life of loneliness. Yes, indeed. The other ministers go home after work and they have their families, their wives. I go home to be alone. I stay celibate. It's an essential of the monastic vocation. It's part of my fidelity to God—and by the same token it's part of my service to the people.

"Recently I published a poem entitled, 'Mystical Vision of the Letters FSLN'—the initials of the Sandinista National Liberation Front. I describe in it an experience of intimate solitude, where I felt God was speaking to me through these letters, showing me what he had done for me and for my people.

"On Motastepe Bluff, you see, in Managua, there used to be a big billboard advertising a brand of shoes, in giant white letters: ROLTER. In my poem I talk about how a boy named Juan asked me what those letters meant. I told him. And he said to me, 'When the revolution wins, there won't be any more ads like that, right?'

"Right!" I said.

"Then the revolution won, time passed, and my promise to Juan was not kept—until one day there appeared on the sign, in big letters, FSLN. I remember that little conversation with Juan often, and joyfully. But here's how the poem ends:

> It was Sunday, and the noonday sky was dour.
> You know, there are days when you ask a sign.
> Lonely, intimate times: as
> when Saint Therese, on her bed of agony,
> wondered if God existed.
> Then from my car I saw the letters,
> great upon the bluff, and within me God spoke:
> "See what I have done for all of you—
>   what I have done for your people.
> See these letters, and doubt me not; have faith,
> you of little faith,
> you little coward.

"Yes, you could say I have a sad life. My consolation is in my people's love. I feel it through and through, whenever I come in contact with them. It's for the people that I do this, it's for the people that I keep up this life of loneliness, and it's a loneliness that will end only when I die."

> *"Our community at
> Solentiname was inspired by
> the spirit instilled in me by
> Thomas Merton."*

"It seems to me," I said to Ernesto, "from what you say, that this present stage in your life can be understood only in the light of what lies behind it—the steps that brought you here, the experiences that have made you the way you are now. What steps, what experiences, led you to become minister of culture?"

"First, I had a religious conversion, in which I discovered God as love. It was an experience of a loving faith, a falling in love. It made me want to live in the most isolated, lonely place I could find, to be alone with God. And I felt that the ideal place

would be a Trappist monastery. So I entered the Trappists.
There I renounced everything, even my interest in poetry and my
interest in politics. And my novice master, Thomas Merton,
showed me that it shouldn't be this way. He showed me that just
because I surrendered myself to God, that didn't mean I was
supposed to change my personality. I should keep being the
same as before, just as interested in what I was interested in
before, interested in the fate of Nicaragua, in Somoza's
dictatorship, and in everything that had been important to me
before.

"Merton didn't just say this to me conceptually, he taught it
to me especially by the way he acted. He was already starting to
get acquainted with Zen, and it seemed to me that he used a Zen
method with me. He would get together with me for a spiritual
conference—then, instead of talking to me about 'spiritual
things,' he'd start asking me about Somoza, or about the
dictator of Venezuela, Pérez Jiménez, or the one in Colombia,
and so on, or about the poets of Nicaragua. Then he would start
telling me about his poet friends. And so our precious 'spiritual
direction' time all went by, 'wasted.' I'm sure he did this
deliberately.

"Merton was very interested in politics, and in all sorts of
social problems. About this same time, too, he had discovered
Gandhi and had become a great Gandhian. He was making
Gandhians of us novices. It was also about this time that he
started being a great proponent of nonviolence in the United
States. He was also very interested in dialogue with Marxists and
was sympathetic with them. This was before Vatican II, before
anybody talked about that.

"I had to leave the Trappists, for health reasons, but Merton
saw this as providential: he was already thinking of founding a
community different from the Trappists in Latin America, and
he wanted to found it with me. As we said goodbye he told me
that if he couldn't leave the Trappists I would found this
community myself, and so I ought to study for the priesthood.
He told me that there was still a great deal of clericalism in the
church, and so, to direct a little foundation, a small community,
it was very important to be a priest, to have more influence.

"So I started studying for the priesthood. I still hoped he'd
get permission to leave the Trappists to found this community,

but I finished my studies and was ordained a priest and he still didn't have permission. So, right after my priestly ordination, I founded the little Solentiname community. The bishop of that region had agreed that I was being ordained a priest to found this community, and not for other pastoral work somewhere else.

"I went to visit Merton for final instructions, and also to get him to write a rule for us. And he told me that the first rule would be that there would be no rule, otherwise there would be no end of rules. He gave me a letter for the pope—for me to take to Rome to get him permission to spend a long period of time in our community as spiritual director—although later he told me that there wouldn't be time for me to deliver the letter. He was still going to come to Solentiname when we heard he'd been electrocuted, by an electric fan, in Bangkok, at a meeting of Eastern contemplatives. He'd just given a talk on monastic life and Marxism.

"Merton had told me many times that the contemplative life would have to 'go political.' That's why he was afraid of starting an official Trappist community in Latin America. He said that those North American monks, with their conservative ideas, and their admiration for Franco, would go along with a dictatorship in Latin America, and maybe the community would be founded in a country with a dictatorship: most had dictatorships anyway. So our Solentiname community, inspired by this spirit of Merton's, was a 'politicized' community right from the start, involved with the Nicaraguan people, and with its liberation. Eventually this brought me into contact with the Sandinista Front."

> *"We joined the FSLN in the revolution. I didn't want to be a government minister. I thought I'd go back to Solentiname, and take up my former life again."*

"First, there was a letter from Tomás Borge, which he sent me from where he was hiding. Tomás said this was the first contact

the Sandinista Front had had with priests, and he invited me to
come to see him. So I had my first talk with him. And afterward
there were other talks, with him and Carlos Fonseca. Later
I went to Cuba, and there I saw that the Cuban revolution
was love for neighbor—the gospel in action, 'efficacious
charity.'

"We were also evolving with respect to our position of
nonviolence. We saw that in Nicaragua an armed struggle was
becoming more and more necessary. We recalled that Gandhi
had said that in certain circumstances his doctrine of
nonviolence couldn't be put into practice—in Hitler's Germany
it could not have been put into practice, and it was the same in
Somoza's Nicaragua. Merton had already died, but I'm sure he
would have thought the same as we.

"About this same time, the current of liberation theology
began to well up in Latin America, and it was gradually
identifying us with our people's revolution, with the Sandinista
National Liberation Front.

"My brother Fernando began to have contact with the leaders
of the Sandinista Front before I did, and it was he who
introduced me to Eduardo Contreras. He tied us in even more
closely with the organization. And in the United States I met
with d'Escoto. He had been waging a hard fight against the
Somoza dictatorship, but he had not yet had contact with the
Front. I was asked to speak to him about a meeting that would
be held in Mexico, and I understand that this was the beginning
of d'Escoto's ties with the Sandinista Front.

"The young men in my Solentiname community had been
wanting to leave for some time now, to go and fight with the
guerrillas in the mountains. I had to hold them back, because if
they left, our community would be destroyed. So I had to make
them see that the community represented something good for
the nation. They were not very convinced, but we received a
message from Eduardo Contreras saying that our community
should be kept going because it had political and military
importance, and tactical and strategic importance, for the
Sandinista Front. We quickly understood what he meant by
military importance when we learned that there was going to be
a Sandinista offensive in which that whole region of the country

would be involved. The offensive would need the participation
of the young Solentiname members as guerrillas. They accepted
the invitation with enthusiasm. They trained, preparing for the
offensive.

"Earlier, I had met with Carlos Fonseca and Tomás Borge.
They had told me they wanted me to be one of the three
members of a government junta; they were sure that the guerrilla
war was about to be won. I was told that I would soon get word
to head for the mountains. But a few months later, Eduardo
Contreras and Carlos Fonseca died, one day apart. Later the
order came from the Sandinista Front for the attack in which the
Solentiname members were to take part, in the city of San
Carlos. Boys took part in this attack and so did girls.

"A few days before, I'd been called out of the country by the
Front. The first task I was given was to handle the formal
introductions of the new government that would be set up.
There was already a government ready and waiting, made up of
the Group of Twelve. So I was the one who formally presented
this new government to Carlos Andrés Pérez, who was president
of Venezuela, and from then on it was one trip after another,
taking me to so many countries.

"I was also appointed spokesperson for the Sandinista Front,
because the others, in their clandestine operations, could not
make public statements to the press or on radio or television. I
kept at this work until the revolution was victorious.

"When the new government was being set up, in Costa Rica, I
received a phone call asking me if I would be minister of culture.
I said I didn't want to, but that if they thought it was necessary I
would agree. They asked me again—did I accept or not? I
repeated that I didn't want to accept, but that if they ordered
me to do it, I would. And again they asked me if I was saying
yes or no. After the third request I answered, 'Then, yes, I
accept'—thinking it would be for three months or so.

"A little later it occurred to me that three months wouldn't be
long enough, and that maybe it would have to be six months.
And the time has been drawn out like that, as circumstances in
the country kept requiring me to continue in this duty. I didn't
ask for it, in fact I had never even thought of it: there was no

ministry of culture before, and Sandinista Front plans never mentioned creation of a ministry of culture. This was a last-minute decision, it would seem. I had thought that I'd just go back to Solentiname, back to my former life."

> *"My obedience is to God's will. We'll never disobey the church."*

"Ernesto, there are some who say that you priests in the government obey the Sandinista Front blindly and that you disobey the church—the hierarchy, the bishops."

"My obedience is to God's will. If, in my case, and in these circumstances, I see that God's will is expressed through the historical conditions of this revolution, then I consider that my belonging to the revolution is my obedience to God. And this doesn't involve any disobedience to the church.

"In the first place, we priests were authorized to hold public office. When I was at the Vatican, the secretary of state, Cardinal Casaroli, told me that the Vatican's stand with respect to priests in political office was well known, but that he considered the Nicaraguan situation an exception because it was something new. In fact, afterward he asked me about Solentiname, and I told him I wanted to go back to Solentiname, and wanted to be relieved of the office of minister of culture soon, because it was a heavy burden for me. Right away I could see his concern, and the first thing he asked me was, Who would replace me as minister? I told him I had no way of knowing.

"We are not being disobedient to the church. We'll never disobey the church. If the church changes its mind and withdraws its authorization to continue in our duties, then, if it doesn't seem right to lay them aside just then, in order not to disobey the church we can always ask for temporary laicization. This is what Camilo Torres did when the cardinal of Colombia ordered him to suspend his political activities and he was sure that he was doing the will of God with those political activities. He requested return to the lay state, in accordance with canon law, so that he could continue his activities. And it was granted. Camilo Torres has never been considered a disobedient priest.''

> *"What do I get out of being minister of culture? Taking up my cross daily. "*

"It's being said in some political and church circles that priests in the government hold their offices for power, for the glory of command and personal advantage. "

"I don't look on it as being in power or having power. The purpose of this revolution is to give power to the people. It's a revolution of popular power, and we're there to serve the people.

"I never look on it as if I'm commanding. I'm serving.

"Usually when someone is removed from political office we say that person has 'fallen.' When I'm no longer minister I won't consider I've fallen; I'll consider I've gone up a few notches. Now, while I'm minister, is when I've 'fallen'; right now is when I'm lower.

"I'm fairly well known abroad, but not as minister of culture. I'm known for my literary work, which I've had to drop almost entirely, with the exception of a very few poems, in order to serve as a government minister. If I were looking for fame, I'd find more of it as a writer than as minister of culture.

"As for money, I receive more in royalties from my books than from my salary as minister. Salaries, even the highest ones, are modest in this revolution. And I give away part of my salary as minister. I don't usually keep accounts, but once out of curiosity I did add things up and I found out I'd lost quite a bit of money in my job as minister. Far from making money, I've actually spent some of the income from my books on my government job.

"So there's no material profit for me in this job—just the profit of knowing I'm doing my duty, and, in my case, I feel, shouldering my cross daily.''

*"You belong to the Sandinista Party and the Sandinista
Assembly. Aren't you betraying your divine and churchly calling
by engaging in party politics?"*

"This is a revolution that has been carried out in the service of
the people and is still serving the people. In serving the
revolution, we're serving the people. The Sandinista party is not
seeking power for its leaders or seeking privileges; what it seeks
and offers are service and sacrifices. Every promotion in the
Sandinista Front means more sacrifice. For me it would be much
more comfortable not to belong to the Sandinista Assembly,
where I spend even more time, a lot more. But this is time
devoted to the welfare of our people.

"In some of the poems I've managed to write recently, I've
recorded the very deep experiences I've had in this office. I
consider that my divine vocation is the vocation of service, of
servant, of 'minister.' And I must offer this service wherever
God asks me to offer it. The will of God is expressed in the
concrete circumstances of one's life—and in my case this is the
way it has been expressed to me. I'd be betraying my vocation if
I refused to make these sacrifices."

> *"It was the gospel of Jesus
> Christ that made a Marxist of
> me."*

*"Another accusation made against you priests in government is
that you trade off the gospel for Marxism—that you've turned
your backs on Christ and are now following Marx."*

"There's no incompatibility between Christianity and
Marxism. They aren't the same thing—they're different—but
they're not incompatible. Christianity and the system called
democracy aren't the same thing, but they're not incompatible.
Again, Christianity and medical science, for example, aren't the
same thing, but they're not incompatible. Marxism is a scientific
method for studying society and changing it. What Christ did
was to present us with the *goals* of social change, the goals of
perfect humanity, which we are to co-create with him. These

goals are a community of brothers and sisters, and love. But he did not tell us which scientific methods to use in order to arrive at the goal. Science has to tell us this—in our case, the social sciences. Some take one science, others another. But if anyone substitutes Marxism for Christianity, that person has made a mistake, just as if he or she were to take any other social science and substitute it for Christianity. Correctly understood, Marxism and Christianity are not incompatible.

"I have said many times that I am a Marxist for Christ and his gospel, and that I was not drawn to Marxism by reading Marx, but by reading the gospel. It was the gospel of Jesus Christ that made a Marxist of me—I've often said this, and it's the truth. I'm a Marxist who believes in God, follows Christ, and is a revolutionary for the sake of his kingdom."

> *"I don't consider myself a politician; I'm a revolutionary."*

"I've read and heard of a challenge, a kind of dare or accusation, leveled at priests in the government. The bishops, too, voiced it in their June 1981 ultimatum. The hierarchy of the church seems to want you to make a clear choice. Define yourselves, they say, in effect. Make your option once and for all: either be priests or be politicians."

"I don't consider myself a politician; I'm a revolutionary. By revolution, I understand the efficacious practice of love of neighbor, in society and individually. Politics, as traditionally understood—parties battling to gain power or keep it—is something of absolutely no concern to me. And I would say that in Nicaragua, those of us who are in this revolution are not politicians. We don't have this vocation.

"Just yesterday I had a visit from some Peruvians who told me that, on a bus in Managua, they'd met a woman who told them that she knew nothing of politics, and that politics didn't interest her. But they began to talk to her about the revolution, and she immediately became very enthusiastic, and started telling them all the good things the revolution had done. And she didn't consider herself a politician, nor did she have any interest in politics. Obviously she didn't identify the revolution with politics. This is the way it is with me too.''

> ***"My religious vocation is that of a contemplative and a prophet. It's a vocation of union with God and service to the people."***

"But, after all, there was a conflict within the church. The bishops' ultimatum, in June 1981, threatened you with penalties unless you laid aside your government offices. Many Christians in Nicaragua supported you—and Christians and theologians in other countries, too. The Vatican forced a settlement, which permitted you to continue in your posts—but the price was not to be able to celebrate the sacraments or the liturgy or engage in any other priestly function. I don't know how you feel about this. The conflict died down, and now it's back again. It's not over."

"For me, there was no conflict of conscience. None at all.

"My bishop, Bishop Pablo Antonio Vega, once wrote to me on the subject of my desire to return to Solentiname—whenever I could, when I no longer have a position in the government. And he told me, no, a priest had to do priestly pastoral work too. The contemplative life and the priesthood are different things, he said. And I agree with him. My vocation has always been that of a monk, not that of a priest. I told you how I studied for the priesthood because Thomas Merton advised me to, so we could found that monastic community. And I founded it immediately after ordination.

"It seems to me that perhaps in the future we could have married priests; we had them in the past. The church has a law of celibacy for priests today, but the priesthood is not theologically incompatible with marriage. But I do consider celibacy necessary for the monastic vocation. You couldn't have a noncelibate monk. The word 'monk' comes from *monos*, Greek for 'alone,' 'solitary.' As the Trappists never tire of repeating, the vocation of a monk is to live 'alone with the Alone'—it's a betrothal with God.

"It's a curious thing they tell about the life of Saint Benedict, that he was fasting and praying for such a long time that they had to go and tell him that it was Easter, the feast of the resurrection, and that he should stop fasting. In other words he hadn't been saying Mass. Or Saint Bernard—he was a monk, but, after seventeen years in a little cell hidden under a staircase, he was called to perform political tasks in royal courts, and he even organized a crusade, so that he then led a very different life from the one he had been leading. I consider that my vocation is still one of seclusion, even though now I too have to flit about pretty much the same way as Saint Bernard, strange as it must have seemed to him.

"The truth is that liturgy is not my calling. It even bored me when I was with the Trappists. I consider my vocation priestly only in the sense of the calling of a prophet. I think that this is a meaning of priesthood that drove Christ to his own priesthood, over and above the simple cultic priesthood of the Old Testament, which Israel had, and which in a way the pagan religions had, with their solemn rites. In the primitive church, no one was called a 'priest.' They were called 'elders,' meaning pretty much what we mean today when we say that someone's 'in charge' of something. Even the Apostles, the first priests in the church, spent all their time in prayer, or union with God, and in the proclamation of the word—evangelization, prophetic activity.

"My religious calling is that of a contemplative and a prophet—not so much in the cultic or liturgical meaning of priesthood. My vocation is one of union with God and service to the people, to build up his kingdom of life in love."

Ernesto gave me copies of two poems in which he declares for celibacy as a personal option for the sake of the kingdom of heaven. One is about two tortoises mating in the Pacific Ocean off the coast of Nicaragua, while Ernesto and some others were fishing for red porgy. The act was done "in the blue sea, under a blue sky," Ernesto writes, and it was "the same act" as has been performed "in the sea for millions of years." And Ernesto was reminded of Matthew 19:12: ". . . And some there are who have freely renounced sex for the sake of God's reign." Here is how his poem ends:

As a tortoise alone in the Pacific,
alone under the sky,
—heaven's betrothed.

In the other poem, Ernesto recounts a dream he had. It is in the form of an apostrophe to Elvis Chavarría, a young man of his Solentiname community who had fallen in battle:

Elvis Chavarría, I dreamt you were alive
on your Fernando Island of Solentiname, island of your
    Mama,
as if you'd not fallen
    in the charge on San Carlos.
And I went out to see
    your new baby son
    as once before I went to see the girl you'd had,
little brown lass.
    (Yours she surely was—
    little copy of you!)
And I envied you this new son—
that you might do what I was denied,
for I had denied myself—
and then I awoke
and remembered you were dead.
And that your Fernando Island
is Elvis Chavarría Island now,
and that you could not have had
this new little son just like you—
no more than I.
    For you were dead, as even I,
though we live, we two.

"I've kept asking them to appoint another minister, and let me go back to Solentiname."

"Are you conscious of a provisional quality in your assignment? That is, do you feel your assignment is an 'exception'?"

"As far as I myself am concerned, I have to say that I considered it purely provisional from the start. It isn't my vocation, and I accepted it in the belief that I'd be relieved soon. It's lasted much longer than I thought, or than I wanted.

"I've kept after the leaders of the revolution to appoint another minister of culture. I've told them I've been in this post long enough, and they ought to let me go back to my life in Solentiname. But they've always said, 'Not yet'—that the revolution still needs me here, that they'll have others prepared later, but right now they need me for the job. I consider that it's God who keeps me here, and I keep hoping it won't be much longer."

"Why?"

"Because this isn't the way I'm inclined. I've another vocation. Especially, I have the vocation of a poet—not minister of culture or any other activist job.

"It's not that I think it goes against my religious or priestly vocation. When I was in Solentiname my friends often told me I was wasting myself—that I could do a lot for the country, by working with the young on a university campus, for example. And I always said that wasn't my vocation, that I wouldn't be any good as an activist. And yet here I am, by force of circumstances.

"This is why I say it's a cross for me. For other priests, it could be their vocation. They aren't made for solitude, silence, a life of seclusion. But this is what my own vocation is."

> *"I practice many forms of prayer, but the truest prayer is to do the will of God."*

"What does this singular experience contribute to your faith? Does it eat away at it, or damage it? Or does it enrich you spiritually?"

"I've never tried to make such a calculation. I simply consider I've been fulfilling the will of God, and nothing else. And if

there's been any damage to my spiritual life—not that I'm aware
of any—then that's God's affair. God put me here.''

"Do you pray? When ? How?"

"I don't like to talk about my prayer. It's a very intimate,
personal thing to talk about—a matter between spouses, you
might say.

"But I can say this. My prayer is a prayer of union. It may not
be very much union, it may be poor union, but it is union. It
seems to me that it's a form of prayer that doesn't appear on the
charts of some of the manuals of contemplative prayer. But in
the Trappists they told us that those charts don't mirror concrete
reality anyway. Every individual person who prays, we were
told, is in a state of personal prayer that's different from the
ones in the classic texts and treatises on prayer.

"My prayer is informal now, of course. I think routine is
good for prayer—keeping it at the same time every day. But I
can't do this now. Jacques Maritain, in the last book he
wrote—at the end of his life, his most conservative book, maybe
even reactionary—still says something pretty radical. He says
that one of the types of contemplative prayer is action. Simply
action. It's prayer, he says, and it's contemplative—one of the
three types of contemplative prayer. For me, right now, my
main prayer is this action, lived in union.

"The duties of the assignment I have right now aren't what I
like best myself, but I offer them to God—especially all those
particularly disagreeable things I have to spend my time on,
which I already told you about. And this offering that I make to
God, very frequently is prayer as well. And even when I don't
offer it, I'm still doing it for God anyway. Even when I don't
make the morning offering, and offer up my whole day,
everything I do all day I'm still doing for God.

"Sometimes we have a dialogue, too—a conversation. I talk
to God, especially when I most need to. God listens, and
sometimes answers me—not in words, but in the concrete details
of my everyday life.

"I think that the most authentic prayer, after all, is doing the
will of God—not wanting anything except what God wants. This

is what Saint John of the Cross insists on so much: indifference to all things else, and union of wills in one single will. This is what he says our union with God should be.

"The great Catholic poet Paul Claudel was the French ambassador in Washington. And he tells the story of how, so often, at official banquets, during frivolous conversations, he would have his rosary between his fingers, under the table. He would say his rosary! When I have to be engaged in these kinds of official activity—where the conversation is without interest for the service of the people—I pray. I'm not under the table with my rosary in my hand, like Claudel, but I'm praying, as he was. I'm not saying the rosary, but I am having Claudel's experience of saying prayers; I'm praying.

"The rosary used to be my favorite prayer. At one time it was my only prayer. I understood very well, back then, what Charles Peguy meant when he said that he'd like to travel all over the world saying rosaries all the time. That was before my conversion experience. Since then, I can't stand saying the rosary. In the seminary I asked permission not to say it, and I was granted this permission. Instead of saying the rosary I was allowed to practice 'mental prayer.' They called it 'mental prayer.' This doesn't seem to me to be the right name for it. It's not mental, it's only prayer without words, or even without thoughts. Sometimes it's 'affective'—that is, it involves emotions or sentiments. At other times it's not—it can be simply a plunge into emptiness, into pure emptiness, and this, the experts say, is the most intimate union with God.

"I've had certain kinds of what you might call 'mystical' experiences. Let's put 'mystical' in quotation marks. Let's say they're 'visions,' in quotation marks. Not visions in the traditional sense of seeing something supernatural, but more like 'illumination' experiences—something you've never 'seen' before, and now all of a sudden you 'see' it, lighted up by a light from inside you.

"In some of my recent poems I've recorded some of these experiences I call 'visions.' One of them I describe in a poem entitled 'Vision of a Face.' I'm depicting a tightly packed group of persons in a little village, very much out of the way, where I went with Sergio Ramírez. I describe how all those faces suddenly turned into a single face for me, the face of the risen

Christ, so that their meeting there became the triumph of life over death. A similar experience is described in a poem where I talk about a Mass, with two thousand young people, in Düsseldorf, Germany. There too, all those faces in that crowd of young men and women changed into the body of the risen Christ for me.''

> *"I think the best way I can be of service to the revolution is as a poet. "*

Here are the two poems Ernesto speaks of—the ones recounting his "visions." The first one took place in Nicaragua.

Vision of a Face

Sun and flags—
    first the anthems,
  sun and slogans,
      posters and orators,
cheers and slogans,
eyes of all colors,
    every hue of skin,
      every lock of hair,
every mouth its own smile, each nose a different one
(the eyes? light of numberless colors framed in white),
hair—long, short, straight, kinky, Afro—
young persons, he's fat, she has a
    little boy, there's a little old woman with a wrinkled face,
      schoolboys,
yellow pants, red blouse, white shirt, red again, blue,
white, olive drab, black, orange, pink, yellow.
And suddenly I saw from the platform a single face
with thousands of smiles and thousands of pairs of eyes
a Face of faces, Body of bodies,
like a telephoto of ten thousand dots.
    A face somewhat blurry, yet with the look of a halo. . . .
(Or was it a sombrero? Or maybe a beret?)
And I saw
    that this flesh-at-one was triumph over death.
The picture-takers flashed their best.

A congregation jam-packed—
   then forth there flashed the oneness of them all!
—the oneness guaranteeing
Victory.

Ecumenical Liturgy, Düsseldorf

So many faces joined together!
   There must be 2,000—young,
thousands of redheads, a field of waving grain,
flashing back the color of stained glass
   the sun projects down here, waving,
waving under the electronic vibrato of a musical wind.
Communion time. I minister to them
   baskets of red bread, and red wine from the Rhine
in vessels of cardboard. So many
   grains of wheat in a single loaf,
   so many grapes, golden red, in this one wine.
All one in song, too.
     So magnified a single song!
How many throats united in the word of this singing!
And . . . all smiling.
How many smiles joined to one another—
as if in one enormous smiling face.
A face of . . . 2,000 faces,
   lighted by the sun of stained-glass windows—
something here of the glory of risen bodies, I reflect.
It's our face that makes us human. Brutes
are faceless.
   (Nor do they distinguish our faces.
A dog knows a million scents—but faces, never.
And we—we tell apart an infinitude of faces.)
Ah, is this not the meaning of
   "to the image and likeness of God"?
This is the "social being" created by God in the beginning—I
   reflect—
   social . . . *one* . . .
     "male and female God created us," created us *one!*
All those faces formed together one face of all
   and a single face of one.

And Düsseldorf now skims across the surface of this planet,
   little by little,
   to Solentiname,
in a unity of petition:
   "Lord, let Nicaragua be everything they dream of there!"
and
   "May there be, in the world, many
   Nicaraguas."

*"Would you serve the revolution better in Solentiname?
Solentiname rebuilt—what a great symbol for the world! When
will you be able to go back there?"*

"I might serve the revolution in Solentiname—not so much by
any activity I might engage in, but simply by practicing my
vocation. I'd try not to have much activity in Solentiname. I
think my predominant calling (not the one God gave me
later)—the one I was born with—is that of poet, and it's as a
poet that I'll be able to render the best service to the revolution.
As I told you, I've many, many things to write, some of them
half written, in rough draft, and they'd be easy to finish now.
And this is something I could do right away."

> *"I couldn't sit writing poetry
> in Solentiname when
> Nicaragua might be invaded at
> any moment."*

"Solentiname is being rebuilt now, and others can see to that
work. There are young persons there, I trained them myself,
working on the reconstruction of Solentiname—and building
new things, too, that weren't there before. The revolution has
created many co-ops there. A school for training *campesino*
leaders is under construction, and a factory for making
educational toys, a dairy, and a cheese factory.
   "Pretty soon they're going to start work on a little village.
The Solentiname residents always lived all over, not all together
in one village. They're planting vegetable gardens and orchards
now. In other words, there's a whole series of things we couldn't
do before the revolution. At the same time, the painting is going

as well as before, or better. And craft houses are going up, as
before.

"When will I be able to go back to Solentiname? I don't
know. I hope it'll be pretty soon. Not too much longer. I know
there's no way right now. Right now, when Nicaragua is so
threatened, we all have to serve the revolution actively. And I
must serve, not just as minister of culture, but especially by
representing the revolution on the international front. The main
thing that has delayed my return to Solentiname is President
Reagan's rise to power. Reagan has made life very complicated
for us Nicaraguans. He won't let us alone. Naturally I couldn't
go writing verses now in Solentiname, right when Nicaragua is in
danger of being invaded from moment to moment. No, I
couldn't."

•

I walked down the staircase, and out into the shade of the
chilamate trees. How like a monk's cell was the minister's office,
I thought. Small, bright, austere, practically bare. A floor of
earthen tiles, with its big, smooth, bright, sober table. Behind
the table, the only thing I had seen that was "the minister's" was
a comfortable white armchair. Around the table were three low,
rustic chairs, of white canvas on a wooden frame. Under the
balcony you could see the colonial facade, and a tree out on the
patio.

On the white walls of the office, a primitivist painting hung,
from Solentiname, along with three rather large portraits of
Sandino, Carlos Fonseca, and Rigoberto López Pérez, the
Nicaraguan poet who had written to his mother, "I have decided
to be the one to put into effect the beginning of the end of this
tyranny." It was López, in 1956, who had killed the dictator
Anastasio Somoza García, shooting him at point-blank range,
whereupon the dictator's National Guard shot López down on
the spot and finished him off where he lay.

Out among the lemon trees, I turned to see the lake, the
mountains, and Momotombo Volcano. Just a little plume of
smoke rose from the pointed crater, and dispersed against the
blue sky. And I thought about Solentiname, where they had
buried Captain Laureano Mairena just the day before—the

young man who had lived with Ernesto in the monastic commune of Solentiname. Laureano, Donald Guevara, Elvis Chavarría, and Felipe Peña were the four young men of Solentiname who had given their lives for the revolution. I spoke with Ernesto about them. I asked him how he felt about these deaths. He found it difficult to reply.

"It's like asking a father about the death of his child," he said. "Laureano was one of my spiritual children, whom I trained at Solentiname. He came when he was nineteen. His family was Protestant, and he asked to become a Catholic. I didn't force him. He told me he was attracted by the revolutionary Christianity we practiced. He wanted to go and be a guerrilla. I held him back as long as I could, but finally I had to let him go. He was very brave. He always served my Mass, and nobody could take this away from him. He told me he could be killed at any moment, because he headed up a group of border guards. What's so admirable about Laureano is that, although he loved life so much, he was not afraid of death."

Ernesto's rich, dark voice sounded sorrowful and mysterious. The absent look in his eyes must have been fixed on Solentiname.

Laureano had brought some commentaries on the Bible with him when he entered Solentiname. In one of them we read:

> And so, just as God cares for the sparrows of the air, and none fall except by God's loving will, so will God care for us as well. We shall fall when we must—or when our fall will serve some purpose, which is really the same as not falling at all.

How meaningful these words are today, sealed as they are by the death of one who used to read them.

There was no shade under the canopy of the bus stop and I waited in the sun. I heard faraway songs to Mary. They would be singing her praises all over Nicaragua this night. The annual novena was closing on the feast of the Immaculate Conception, traditionally the favorite and most congenial feast of Nicaraguans. It was December. The rains were over and gone, heaven was a brilliant blue, and a spring breeze cooled the sun's hot lash.

"I am a priest forever. And I'll stand by my people to the death."

Fernando Cardenal, National Vice-Coordinator of the Sandinista Youth Movement

Fernando Cardenal was born on January 26, 1934, in Granada, Nicaragua, just after his brother Ernesto's ninth birthday. He went to primary and secondary school with the Jesuits of Granada and himself entered the Society of Jesus on May 19, 1952, at the Santa Tecla novitiate in El Salvador.

Upon completion of his two-year noviceship, Fernando was sent to Ecuador, where he spent the next seven years studying the humanities and philosophy at the Catholic University of Quito. The teaching years of his scholasticate were spent in Nicaragua and Guatemala, from 1961 to 1964. He then studied theology in Mexico, where he was ordained in 1967.

Two years later Father Fernando was in "tertianship," the Jesuit third year of probation or last year of the regular course of studies, in a poor quarter of Medellín, Colombia. This was a most important experience for him and resulted in an irrevocable commitment on his part to the liberation of the poor.

Returning to Nicaragua in July 1970, he was appointed vice-rector of the Central American University, in Managua. But then, in December of that same year, he was expelled from the university for supporting a student strike, whose demands Father Fernando had deemed just. Now he devoted himself to conducting retreats and cursillos, especially for youth.

In April 1973, he founded the Revolutionary Christian Movement, which would supply so many leaders of the Sandinista Front, the FSLN, later on. Around this same time he was appointed to the chair of philosophy of the Autonomous University of Nicaragua.

In June 1976, Fernando traveled to the United States, where he had been asked to testify before a congressional committee concerning Somoza's government in Nicaragua. There he roundly denounced not only the crimes of General Somoza, but those of the United States foreign policy as well. Upon his return to Nicaragua the Somoza regime forbade him to make any more trips abroad.

In 1976 he founded the Nicaraguan Commission for Human Rights. In October 1977, now a member of the Sandinista Front, he secretly left the country for San José, Costa Rica, where he joined the patriots who were to found the Group of Twelve. From now on Fernando Cardenal was totally involved in the struggle against Somoza and his regime.

After the victory of the Sandinista people's revolution, in August 1979, he was named national coordinator of the Crusade for Literacy, which reduced the illiteracy rate in Nicaragua from 51 to 12 percent.

Since September 1980, Father Cardenal has been a member of the Sandinista Assembly and vice-coordinator of the National Executive Committee of the July Nineteenth Sandinista Youth movement.

•

I first met Jesuit Father Fernando Cardenal in San José, Costa Rica, on July 2, 1977. I had come to interview him for the Spanish weekly, *Vida Nueva*. Father Cardenal had been in Costa Rica for ten months now, in "militant exile" from his native Nicaragua, and we held our meeting in the cathedral. Two days later he was to return to his own country, with the other members of the Group of Twelve, to beard General Somoza in his den—to lead a popular insurrection against the dictator and his National Guard.

"We may die," Fernando told me that day. I asked him whether there was not, after all, some conflict between his vocation as a Jesuit priest and his political involvement in the people's liberation movement. His work seemed to me surely to involve a high degree of emergency and risk. Today I easily grasp the intimate connection between the answer he gave me in San José, two years before the victory, and the following lengthy account I recorded in Managua three and one half years after that victory.

This time, I spent an afternoon with Fernando in his Jesuit community. We sat in a kind of parlor, in two big rocking chairs, looking out on the relaxing green of the little garden, with its plants and flowers and a tall acacia they ringed. At the door of Fernando's own room there was a jasmine bush, just beginning to bloom. We talked the afternoon away. The sun disappeared, and night came upon us, as it comes in the tropics—swiftly, hastily.

Fernando is taller and more athletic than his brother Ernesto. His voice is deep too, but of a finer timbre. He speaks with ease, volubility, and passion.

> *"I've always had the vocation to work with youth."*

I asked Fernando, "What has your work been in the revolution since the victory?"

"Two weeks after the triumph of our revolution I was named national coordinator of the Crusade for Literacy. I worked on this project, full-time, for a year. It involved practically half the Nicaraguan population.

"When the Crusade for Literacy was over, I asked to be given something to do with the July Nineteenth Sandinista Youth Movement—the official name of the youth organization of the Sandinista Front. The governing junta had wanted to appoint me vice-minister of education for adult education, which would have been a logical continuation of my work in the literacy campaign. But I insisted that instead of being vice-minister of as grand and glorious a project as our adult education program, I just wanted to keep on working in what I had always done, even before I was ordained: youth work. I wanted to work with revolutionary youth, the Nineteenth of July Sandinista Youth.

"So I joined this project instead, as a member of the National

Executive Committee—the nine of us who headed the Sandinista Youth program. Each of us is in charge of a national secretariat. I'm the national secretary for political training and propaganda of the Sandinista Youth.

"These are the two public posts I've held since the triumph of the revolution."

"You're a religious and a priest, Fernando. You're a Jesuit. Do these assignments you have in the revolution really fit in with your personal state of life? Do you live your vocation in them, without any contradiction? Or do they rather create conflicts of conscience for you? What's your personal experience in this whole respect?"

"The work I'm doing poses no contradiction whatever with the religious training I've received, from the Jesuit novitiate up to the present time. I'm carrying out a task that's in complete accord with my theology, my spirituality, my priesthood, and all that's deepest in my Christian and human sentiments. It's certainly in complete accord with my conscience. To my understanding, this is how our Lord is asking us to be his witnesses and ministers in the conditions our Christian poor live in in Latin America—in our case, in Nicaragua. I'll try to explain, because you've asked me to elaborate on my personal experience.

"As a Jesuit, during my training that lasted seventeen years, I was always orientated toward education. But ever since the first experiences of my teaching years in the scholasticate—in 'regency,' when we leave our studies and go off to work in a school—my orientation has been toward pastoral work with youth rather than toward teaching. And so youth ministry became the goal of my studies and my training for the priesthood quite early. And when I was ordained, I saw the priesthood as a tool for a more effective pastoral ministry with youth, which I'd been devoting myself to since long before ordination.

"I feel very deeply that this whole long stage of preparation, and this orientation of my priestly apostolate toward youth ministry, have been perfectly consistent with what I'm doing right now. I feel that that whole training and direction—that is, my vocation—is emptying out onto what I'm now doing here, because I'm devoting myself to training these young people, I'm working in an organization that welds together a good 17 percent of the high-school population of the country in an organized fashion. Some 30 percent—fifty thousand youths—participate in our activities.''

> *"I do with these young people*
> *what a missionary does in*
> *'pre-evangelization.' "*

"In my work with these young people, I live with the same apostolic attitude as a missionary priest in a mission country where he's been sent and where he has to devote some years of his life to the work of pre-evangelization. During this stage he doesn't explicitly talk about Christ or the faith. He 'speaks' by the witness of his life, by his presence, by his dedication to applying Christ's love present in his faith—by enhancing the humanity of this missionary world he's been sent to. He speaks via his commitment to teaching, educating, and human betterment. Sometimes he's a teacher, sometimes he's an infirmarian, sometimes he's a doctor. Or maybe he helps build homes. It's a stage that's clearly defined in missiology as the stage of 'pre-evangelization,' or human betterment—and it's an integral part of evangelization, as Pope Paul VI points out in his magnificent *Evangelii Nuntiandi*.

"I'm working in a political organization for youth. But my presence there as a priest has a pastoral and ecclesial importance over and above the performance or nonperformance of activities that are directly and explicitly priestly. My presence here, as a priest, is that of a pastoral sign. It's true I don't usually go around talking about the faith. I don't say Mass in my office, or in the halls of the youth organization. And God's name doesn't come up much in the course of my working day. But in the Society of Jesus we're trained to orientate our presence, in the purely secular or scientific work to which we devote ourselves (and numerous Jesuit priests are dedicated to such work), toward the upbuilding of the kingdom of God.

"There are Jesuit priests who spend their lives teaching algebra, and nobody goes running up to them to tell them that that's not priestly. I myself, before I joined the revolution full-time, was a professor of philosophy in the national university. I fulfilled my vocation by teaching the ideas of Plato, Aristotle, Descartes, and Kant, without its having any explicit relationship with my priesthood. And I never thought that this was somehow in contradiction with my priestly state. I never felt frustrated in my courses, I never had a guilt complex just because I devoted myself to something not explicitly 'priestly.' I saw that these courses, too, were part of the church's whole effort to further the coming of the kingdom of God.

"I see my work with the Sandinista Youth Movement as even more germane to that effort, much more consistent with it in fact. I see it, and experience it, live it, as being much more clearly oriented toward the coming of the kingdom. In working with these young persons, in their training for love and service to the people, and to the poorest of the poor, even though it's a political organization, I feel myself more fulfilled as a priest than when I was expatiating on the thought of Leibnitz.

"I have not found, in this work I now do with youth, the least contradiction, inconsistency, or conflict of conscience with the orientation I had all the way through my Jesuit training. The work I'm doing now does not deviate in the slightest from the direction my life has been following for thirty years, from the first day I entered the novitiate of the Society of Jesus."

> *"I used to be concerned that there might be souls in hell. Now I'm concerned with the hell of misery suffered by millions of my brothers and sisters."*

"I entered the Jesuit novitiate because I wanted to serve the people. I was fired with the ideal of devoting my whole life to the service of human beings, and I had discovered what was the most important thing in the world: the salvation of souls, eternal salvation. In the *Spiritual Exercises* of Saint Ignatius, I had seen, in those meditations of his on the four last things, there was not just the danger that I would be condemned myself, but above all the danger that there were so many others on their way to this condemnation. And the apostolate I envisioned in their service, so that they would not finish their lives in such a disastrous way, was for me the most beautiful purpose anyone could devote a life to.

"I entered the novitiate thirty years ago, and all through these thirty years my life has been directed toward the service of my fellow human beings. And the final goal has always been the same: to be of service to the salvation of human beings in the way that God wills. But in the last years of my training I gained a deeper understanding of the danger that so many could end their lives in hell: I came to see that many of them had already begun their hell on earth, as with so many millions of Latin Americans and the misery they're suffering. And so, without altering the basic orientation of my life in the slightest, I began to be concerned with the most urgent kind of service that can be rendered here in Latin America: the service of the integral salvation of human beings and the coming of God's kingdom—the service of the liberation of the poor, here among my people, their humane, economic, social, and political liberation, which is an anticipation and commencement of their integral liberation and the coming of the kingdom. In other words, with liberation from poverty and oppression, the kingdom of God has already begun to emerge, and one day it can reach its fulness."

> *"I've always been able to count on my community and my superiors. This has given me confidence that I'm doing God's will."*

"I also have to say that none of my work or activities, including my political involvement and my part in my people's struggle, has ever drawn me away from my religious community. Always, in all the decisions I've made over the course of these years—from when I first started working with the Sandinista

Front for National Liberation—I've always been able to count on my community and my superiors. Basically these decisions were always made in consultation with my fellow Jesuits and my superiors; we made our analyses and evaluations together.

"This evaluation process, or 'community discernment' with respect to the work each of the members of a Jesuit community is doing, has been a constant practice with us. I remember when I was teaching in the national university, in one of the most important evaluations we ever made, all the members of our community presented what they were doing in their work, all their activities, and the rest of the community evaluated it from the apostolic and Jesuit point of view. So I presented my work, as a teacher in the university. And then I listened to what my confreres had to say to me, to see if I should keep doing what I was doing, or devote myself to something else.

"Every one of them agreed that the very fact that I was the only priest in Nicaragua working in the national university was an apostolic labor in itself. They all said that the fact that I would be walking down the corridor and others would say, 'There goes Father Cardenal, he's a priest, and he's involved in the people's liberation struggle'—this was already known, all over Nicaragua—just the fact that my presence was reminding others at the university that a priest, or a Christian, can and should be committed to the struggle of his or her people, was a sermon in itself, a testimonial. My confreres said it was important that I should continue in this work. Of course, in class I didn't talk about the gospel; I had to talk about Plato.

"My confreres gave me their complete support in this work, just as they support me completely now in my work with the members of the Sandinista Youth Movement. It's the same sort of thing. In their view, giving a course on a secular subject in the university was actually an apostolic activity, in accordance with my vocation as a priest and a Jesuit, because of the witness of a life of involvement with and commitment to the poor. Likewise, now, they view my presence in the Sandinista Youth Movement as apostolic work as well. The fact that students, in the midst of everything they may hear or see about the revolution, or Marxism, or atheism—the fact that they also know and see that there's a priest among them, and that he's the director of this youth organization but that he's still a priest, loyal to his faith and his priesthood, is a sermon in itself, a witness, an ecclesial and pastoral sign.

"And so, in the work I do here, I feel not only the personal satisfaction of performing an activity that's consonant with my priestly and religious state, but the great satisfaction of knowing that my community supports me in this work as well. I know my community understands my work, and is in favor of it, and values it. In their view, this work of mine is a work of great apostolic importance: the church, through a priest, is present to the Sandinista youth. And knowing they think this is a great support to me.

"This is what I mean when I say that maintaining communion with my religious community and my superiors, in this work I do, strengthens and crowns the deep satisfaction I have in carrying out my religious vocation of service to my people with this work of the revolution. It means I'm doing God's will. In the religious life, the approval and encouragement of one's community and superiors has always been the sign and means of knowing that one is fulfilling the will of God."

*"The Crusade for Literacy
was in the direct line of the
works of mercy."*

"What I've just been saying I've seen come true, ever so clearly, in the work I did in the revolution even before I started my job with the Sandinista Youth Movement. I was national coordinator of the Crusade for Literacy. De facto this was a political project, planned and executed because the leaders of the revolution had the 'political' intent—in the sense of the intent to serve the common good—to keep their promise to the people and start a process of democratization. This process of democratization called for the participation of all the popular classes, the masses of the people, in directing the history of Nicaragua. But this participation, in turn, demanded as a first step that the illiterate half of the Nicaraguan population learn to read and write and begin a process of education. Then all those Nicaraguans would be able to participate in the political process.

The leaders of the revolution wanted to fulfill this political commitment to their people, and they put me in charge of making it a reality.

"I began to direct the literacy crusade, not by dividing myself in half—not by saying, 'Now I'm going to do the job the revolution's given me and leave my priesthood back there in my community'—no, I began to do this work precisely as a priest integrated into the revolution. I was not divided between revolution and priesthood. And I felt the great satisfaction of the revolutionary who sees that, after victory, the situation of the people changes—that the people begins to take its destiny into its own hands and goes on to build a new country, for the new humanity to live in. And at the same time, as a priest I felt the deep satisfaction that this work was in direct line with what our Lord asks of us in the gospel—that it is in the direct line of what we call the works of mercy, the things we're called on to do to prepare for the coming of the kingdom of God.

"In Saint Matthew's Gospel, in chapter 25, beginning with verse 31, we read what the last judgment will be like. And there's a commandment there, an order given—a very clear directive. It's that we're to be concerned with feeding the hungry, clothing the naked and the barefoot, and teaching the ignorant. Fifty-one percent of all Nicaraguans were illiterate. So they had to be taught to read and write. Well, I was right in the thick of it as priest-coordinator of the national Crusade for Literacy. And when we started visiting the whole country, and seeing the enthusiasm of the peasants as they started to feel the revolution's concern and love coming all the way to them, and when the whole country started 'going to school'—this enormous school of almost a million persons—well, nobody could tell me I wasn't doing priestly work. Quite the contrary.

"Besides, I was doing something incorporated in the Constitutions of the Society of Jesus. Saint Ignatius wrote that when anyone is appointed rector or provincial, he's supposed to set aside some time to instruct the *rudi,* the ignorant. And he labeled this work with the ignorant a very important task, to which we Jesuits were always to devote some time. And all of a sudden the revolution gave me the chance to coordinate the work of teaching nearly a million illiterate Nicaraguans to read!

How could I not feel priestly and religious satisfaction in doing this? That whole year, which was devoted to teaching our people to read, I was right where the gospel wants us to be, right where a priest should be.

"One fellow Jesuit of mine, a priest who'd taught me when I was in school—he's about seventy years old now—was a ham radio operator. He joined the literacy crusade with me, all fired up like a sixteen-year-old. He had incredible energy. Day and night, he was in charge of the radio communications network—for all types of services and emergencies, sometimes serious, like rescuing persons in accidents, or transporting the sick or dying and then getting in touch with their families. After the crusade was over, when this priest had gone back to the school where he'd spent his whole life as a math teacher, he told me, 'Never, as long as I live, will I ever again do anything as important as that. Nothing in my life has ever given me the satisfaction that that work in the national Crusade for Literacy did.' He'd studied theology in the first quarter of this century. And yet his deep human sensitivity and spiritual intuition enabled him to grasp perfectly well what was so evangelical about being tied down to a microphone twenty-four hours a day—at the service of thousands of teachers, all over the country, who'd thrown themselves into teaching our people to read and write.

"And I want to tell you something else. It isn't just my work with literacy, or my work with youth, that gives me a life so in keeping with my priestly and religious state. It's my whole political participation in this revolution. Sometimes you can study so many things. You can read book after book. And all of a sudden one day you find, couched in a simple phrase, something that illuminates everything you've been reading and studying. I remember a phrase like that in the Medellín documents. It says that political activity is the 'noblest and most efficacious form of practicing charity.'

"Then besides, there are emergency situations—'exceptional' historical considerations—in this country to compel and oblige a person to political work as a matter of necessity, as an evangelical duty. The work, the assignments we priests are given in this revolution in Nicaragua ought not to be measured by the same standards as political work and assignments in other parts of the world—in countries such as Italy, for instance, or Spain, France, Germany, Switzerland, or the United States, or Canada, or so many other countries. To me this seems important and basic.

"With all the threatening circumstances here, with the threat of invasion, economic crisis, economic and news blockade— after all we've gone through and suffered here in Nicaragua—after all it's cost us to break free of our slaveries and dependencies and be a free people, which God has certainly wanted, and still wants us to free ourselves from—I feel that my work is a perfectly honorable and effective service, a way of demonstrating and acting out my Christian love for my people, with so many and such serious needs."

> *"In Medellín, among the poor, I came to understand that God isn't neutral. And I swore to live for their liberation."*

"You say that what you're now doing is consistent with your whole Jesuit formation, with your conscience, and with your priestly dedication in the thirty years you've been in the Society of Jesus. Would you expand on this a bit? What are the convictions and experiences that have given you this certainty—that oblige you to get politically involved in this revolution as a duty of the gospel and the priesthood?"

"I entered the novitiate in 1952. I don't think anything particularly important happened for the answer to your question until 1969, when my theological studies were over and I was already a priest. That was when I moved to Medellín, Colombia, for the last year in my Jesuit training.

"I already had a concern for what we called the 'social problem,' but it was in an abstract and romantic way that wasn't translated into anything concrete. I think the first concrete translation was precisely my asking to go to Medellín instead of to Spain, which was a big attraction for me because I'd never been to Europe.

"I knew that the tertian master in Medellín was Father Miguel Elizondo, a Spanish Jesuit of our province who was always starting something new. And now he'd just moved the tertianship from a very beautiful building surrounded by gardens—a very comfortable, large, five-story building in a city called La Ceja, outside Medellín—to a very poor neighborhood in Medellín. That way those of us who went there to do tertianship would be living for nine months in the midst of the poverty of a typical Latin American popular neighborhood, among the poor.

"This decision changed my whole life. Living with the poor, in that slum, taught me, in a practical, daily, very difficult way, the crass reality of how millions of Latin Americans actually live. And the ties of friendship, affection, and love that I was able to form with the people who lived in that slum, the discovery I made of their magnificent human values, right in the midst of the violation and deprivation of their rights, made their situation something I finally couldn't stand any more.

"The intense spiritual training of those nine months set me to study and deepen what I'd seen in theology in the form of tractates and manuals that prepared you for an exam, but now was my daily bread, and a response to my restlessness. And so I began to discover that in the Christian priesthood there was not just the cultic, or liturgical, aspect—which was the only thing the Old Testament priesthood had actually been—but that Christ had inserted into the priesthood a prophetic aspect. It was an aspect whereby the Christian priesthood was supposed to make its other aspects prophetic as well—the cultic or liturgical, and the pastoral. I saw that the Christian liturgy should be prophetic—that it should boldly proclaim salvation in Christ and denounce everything opposed to that salvation: all sin, all injustice, all human selfishness that offended God in his living image—when the masses of a nation are made to suffer the misery that results from sin, selfishness, and social injustice, for example.

"And so in the course of almost three hundred days—days of prayer, study, contact with misery, contact with the poor, contact with those who live with exploitation, eviction, and hunger, in filth, in a slum without any electricity or any other

municipal services or utilities—I came to understand the
message of the prophets and the message of Jesus: that the God
who's revealed himself to us in the Bible isn't a neutral God, but
a God who takes sides with the poor. And therefore we, as
priest-prophets of the church of the New Testament, can't be
neutral either.

"This was decisive for my life. Those slum-dwellers wanted
me to stay with them after the nine months of my tertianship
were over, stay in Medellín. But I felt I couldn't do anything for
them. Their basic problem was eviction from their lands, and I
didn't know anything about Medellín or anybody there; I
couldn't find them work or change their situation. But I did
know that if I went back to Nicaragua I would certainly be able
to do something—something that would not only help the poor
of Nicaragua but all the exploited peoples of Latin America.
Before I left their shantytown in Medellín, I swore to them I'd
devote my life, all the life left to me, to fighting for the
liberation of the poor. This was in 1970, in July.

"When I went back to Nicaragua, then, I carried with me
a very clear and concrete idea of what our last general
congregation had already told us Jesuits in no uncertain terms:
that we were to devote our lives to the propagation of the faith
and the defense of justice—both of them perfectly integrated
into a single flow of activity.

"Three days after I took office as vice-rector, in charge of the
students in the Central American University—a university
conducted by the Jesuits here in Managua—the students went on
strike and took over the university. And when I heard the speech
by one of the student leaders, explaining their demands, I could
see that the requests they were making of the rector and the
university administration were just. What I did not have an
inkling of was that, when this student leader had finished
speaking, he was going to announce that they would now have a
few words from the new vice-rector! And they passed me the
megaphone.

"Standing there with the megaphone in my hand, I knew I
had to make an instantaneous decision. I was going to have to
choose between loyalty to the rector, who had been my friend
ever since I was a child and was the spiritual director to whom I

owed my vocation, and loyalty to my conscience—to truth and justice, which were on the students' side. I told the students that what they sought seemed just to me—so I would support them, as long as they sought it in a just way, did not give up, and fought until they had it, because it was right.

"This cost me expulsion from the university. It cost me the loss of the friendship of my fellow priest, the rector. But I had to do it, because of the oath I'd sworn to the slum-dwellers in Medellín. What the university students were demanding were not the demands of the masses of the poor. But they were united in one cause, the cause of justice, the cause of the weak. The students were not poor, but they were weak, and they cried out for justice."

> *"I saw that the FSLN was the good Samaritan rescuing wounded Nicaragua. I couldn't refuse them without offending God."*

"Then I began doing a number of things in support of activities for justice, activities on behalf of the exploited, which were taking place in the country at that time: demonstrations in favor of the teachers persecuted by the dictator Somoza, hunger strikes, the seizure of the cathedral to demand the release of political prisoners belonging to the Sandinista Front who were being tortured and slaughtered by Somoza in the prisons. Speeches, magazine articles, and all sorts of public demonstrations were already demanding justice at that early, peaceful stage. Nicaraguans had begun to make public demands for justice and change in their country. They wanted change not only with respect to the person of the dictator, but a change in the socio-economic structures that held the majority of the population in repression.

"As a result of this public activity, in 1970, I was called on by Comandante Oscar Turcios (later murdered by Somoza's National Guard, in 1973) to be a member of the national administration of the FSLN. We talked about it. Although I did not join the Sandinista Front at that time, that conversation

influenced me a great deal, and all my work took on a greater
sense of commitment. I came to see more deeply and
realistically, with each passing day, that the country no longer
had any option but armed struggle. I was and still am a great
admirer of Gandhi and Martin Luther King, Jr., and I had
hoped to help get their sort of nonviolent struggle under way in
Nicaragua. I took part in hunger strikes, demonstrations, sit-ins,
and all sorts of nonviolent campaigns. But I came to realize that
it was too late.

"In 1973, Comandante Eduardo Contreras—introduced to
me at that time simply as 'Marcos'—asked me to work with the
Sandinista National Liberation Front. At once I recalled the
gospel parable of the good Samaritan and meditated on it in
depth. For me now, there was no doubt but that there were, in
Nicaragua, a group of persons called the Sandinista National
Liberation Front, who had stayed with our wounded people, this
nation wounded by exploitation and misery. This people lay by
the side of the road, and the FSLN was the good Samaritan,
caring for that wounded victim. There was no doubt in my mind
that this was the way things were. And Marcos was saying to me,
in effect: 'Fernando, we're asking you to help us care for this
slaughtered, tortured, exploited people, living in misery,
malnutrition, and illiteracy.'

"In a matter of seconds, I understood, profoundly and
altogether clearly, that I couldn't refuse without offending God.
I saw, with perfect transparency, that I couldn't do as the priest
and the Levite and simply pass by. I understood that all my
preparation and training, from high-school graduation on, as I
tried to serve others and tried to see how in the Society of Jesus
and the priesthood I could serve my fellow human beings—all
this had to be made concrete now, right now, in one, single yes,
once and for all. God was asking me to cooperate in the care and
salvation of this wounded people. The hour had come to fulfil
the vow I'd made to the poor of that Medellín slum. And I said
yes, they could count on me . . . irrevocably yes.

"I reported that decision to my community, and all of
them—including fellow Jesuits who'd come from Spain—agreed
that, as a Nicaraguan religious and priest, I'd made the right
option.

"From then on my work became more committed, and more

dangerous. Now I was involved in both public and clandestine activities in preparation for the final insurrection. I worked with Comandante Tomás Borge and Comandante Daniel Ortega, and I was in contact with Comandante Bayardo Arce—all members of the national administration of the FSLN—and especially with Comandante Eduardo Contreras, who was murdered in 1976. The work they had me do involved physical risk, in fact it involved laying my life on the line, because torture and murder were always just around the corner in those days. All arrests began with torture. Interrogation came afterward.

"In 1977, Comandante Daniel Ortega asked me to join the Group of Twelve, the political group to be formed in Costa Rica in October. I hadn't been allowed out of the country for a year now, since my return from the United States, where I'd testified before a congressional committee and made a public denunciation of the crimes of the Somoza dictatorship. I'd accused the president of the republic, General Anastasio Somoza, of murder, torture, and theft. From then on I wasn't allowed out of the country, so I had to sneak out through the mountains and join the others in San José, Costa Rica. Now I was devoting all my time to the work of preparing for the insurrection, which came in September 1978, the final offensive of 1979, and victory on July 19, 1979, the day when our revolution succeeded in overthrowing and expelling Somoza and his army."

> *"I didn't meet with the slightest objection on the part of my superiors or the bishops to my participation in the struggle."*

"Did you have any problems, or were there any criticisms or warnings from your community and your superiors, or from the bishops, with regard to your political activities with the FSLN from 1973 until victory in July 1979?"

"As far as the Jesuits were concerned, I had no problem. None. My work, my commitment, my struggle were always considered an exceptional service, a necessary, urgent service to a people being slaughtered. I recall a father provincial saying that the situation in Nicaragua had come to such a pass that anything anybody might do to save this nation and its people would be completely justified. I kept in communication with the provincials I had during this period, and major decisions were always made in consultation with them.

"As far as the bishops were concerned, they never had the slightest reservation either, in spite of the fact that my position and my activity opposing the regime were quite public. My activities were well known. The government described them as part of the guerrilla struggle, or 'terrorism and communism,' as they called it. Everyone in Nicaragua knew that everything we did was in the service of the Sandinista Front, although we didn't say so publicly for fear of our lives.

"When I accused Somoza and his regime of murder to the U.S. Congress, the lists of the missing, the tortured, and the murdered I presented were all of peasant collaborators of the FSLN. The only names I gave were those of poor, lowly mountaineers, up where the guerrillas were. I did this to make things still clearer, and to be able to give an answer when I would be asked, 'Fernando, for whom were you speaking when you spoke to the U.S. Congress?' The members of the committee did ask me this question. And I told them the truth: 'I am here in the name of the barefoot, lowly peasants of Nicaragua.'

"But in Nicaragua the question became more specific: '. . . Defending the barefoot and the lowly, to be sure—but in the name of what organization?' And here the only possible answer was 'the FSLN.' From 1976 on there could be no doubt that my work was connected with the Sandinista Front. And never, in all this time, was anything at all said to me, or any objections raised.

"I even went to speak personally with Archbishop Obando before going to the United States. My denunciations in the U.S.A. were going to have repercussions in the church, so my bishop, the archbishop of Managua, was one of the few persons I told what I was going to do. And when I came back I went to him again, to tell him how it all had gone. It seemed to me that it was my duty as a priest to go and tell him. And at no time did he raise any objection to what I was doing.

"In 1977, then, I was part of the Group of Twelve, which publicly defended the FSLN. And we turned up in Nicaragua in July 1978, as a group, and paid a visit to Archbishop Obando. Two of us in the group were priests—Father Miguel d'Escoto and I. And neither in the course of that visit nor during the months to come before the final insurrection did the archbishop at any moment, either directly or indirectly, say anything that might be construed as imposing a limitation on us or as reflecting any reservations on his part as to what we were doing, so as to suggest that it would be inappropriate for us to continue doing it for pastoral reasons, canonical reasons, or any other reasons.

"I stayed in contact with my superiors, both with the superior of my local community and with my provincial. Sometimes I even asked the provincial to come and see me secretly, so that I could speak with him. He never had the slightest objection, reservation, or animadversion to make about my activity. I always had the approval of all my superiors."

> *"It's not a matter of having power yourself. It's a matter of making it possible for the poor to have power."*

"Why didn't you priests drop your political activity once the revolution was victorious?"

"Because we saw that the struggle wasn't over. The struggle was entering a new, decisive stage, which was going to be very hard. The tyrant and his National Guard had been overthrown—but reconstruction and the transformation in depth of the whole system and its structures had yet to be begun. Now we could start improving the conditions of our poor population, and it seemed to us that we'd all be needed. There were few enough of us. We considered we'd all, priests included, be needed to start, and then move ahead with, the enormous tasks that lay before us. The tasks we were going to have to do seemed to us in no way inconsistent with our religious and priestly state.

"Our commitment to the people didn't stop with the triumph over Somoza. It was strengthened, it was consolidated. It was deepened. Our new project with the people was going to have to have a lot of support; it was very shaky at first and had to suffer enormous harassment from powerful forces. And yet it was necessary, it was the cause of justice. Supporting this cause, this 'forward march of the people,' didn't mean having power yourself, power as a sign of privilege. It meant bolstering the possibilities for the poor to have power.

"We had to keep on in the struggle for the 'new society' and the 'new march forward of the people.' It was up to us priests to keep Christian values and ecclesial values present in the revolution. There we were, face to face with the possibility that, for the first time in history, a revolution might establish a socialism that wouldn't be anti-Christian or anticlerical, and that Christianity and the church wouldn't turn away from it and be its adversary. But this historic possibility was so threatened, so tenuous. It could so easily abort. How we hoped it would not! And so we offered to help prepare the next step in the work too."

"Many of those who may have approved of what you priests were doing in the early stages of the struggle against Somoza now disapprove of it. They think the Sandinista Front has changed, betrayed, the original program of the people's revolution."

"In fact, it's very easy to see that the Sandinista undertaking, the Sandinista program, with all the support it had from so many countries of Latin America and Europe when it was fighting to overthrow the Somoza government, is still substantially the same today. The basic goals and values that united so many persons in this country, of all social classes, in the struggle against the Somoza dictatorship stand unshaken.

"All the basic, novel elements of this process are still there. What's changed is not the program of the Sandinista Front, but the fact that, in the years of the struggle against Somoza in Nicaragua, all elements of the people were united in that struggle. Even the rich were with us.

"In 1973, immediately after the earthquake, General Somoza began to enter into hot business competition with the rich. And a greedy competitor he was. Insatiable. He monopolized every possible means to get his own business enterprises in the most favorable position, as they competed with the initiatives of all private enterprise. So the FSLN had everybody with them in the fight against Somoza.

"But once Somoza, along with his whole army, fell, and the Sandinista Front began to run the government with great moderation and started putting in practice the reforms that were needed to really transform this country so that it favored the masses of the poor, then these changes, these reforms, started to hit the rich in their pocketbooks—hit them very gently, in fact, very prudently, but started to hit them. And this was when the rich started opposing the Sandinista revolution, claiming that it had 'betrayed the program.' The only thing the rich had wanted, of course, was a change in figureheads—not a change in the system.

"Unfortunately, religious elements have also sounded an echo, not of the Easter gladness of a people reaching the end of its exodus and beginning to reconstruct its land of promise, but an echo of sorrow and protest of those who are pining for their privileges—privileges that they had held for centuries and that they are now gradually having to yield to the interests of a society where everybody is to be privileged.

"To me the case is clear. It's not that the Sandinista Front has betrayed any of its principles. It's the wealthy, and those who have catered to them out of self-interest, who are calling the revolution into question. And they're not calling it on the carpet for abandoning the revolution the Sandinista Front planned, but precisely for carrying out what it planned: the transformation of the country—land reform and structural reforms to make Nicaragua a country where justice reigns, a community of brothers and sisters."

"However that may be, there is, de facto, a conflict in the church over public offices held by priests in the revolution—a conflict that's reached the highest hierarchical echelons of the church. In June 1981, the bishops of Nicaragua published their

*ultimatum: priests would either abandon their government posts
or be punished. Then the Vatican applied the brakes, and the
bishops permitted you to continue in your posts, provided you
renounced the exercise of your priestly functions.*

*"Now the matter is in the forefront again. Word is out that
the Vatican is pressuring you to leave your government
positions. It's said that Father Dezza, the vicar of the Society of
Jesus, the personal delegate of Pope John Paul II, is exerting his
authority on the Jesuits in this matter. How do you, Fernando,
feel about this conflict?"*

"I have to admit that all sorts of indications like this have
been in the wind since 1980, back when I was in the literacy
crusade. Even then there were rumors of our having to abandon
our tasks and services to the people in the revolution. I always
perceived them as motivated by a political view of things. Never
at any moment did I sense a truly pastoral and evangelical
concern for us personally as priests, or for the mission of the
church to the people, or for the kingdom of God. I'm not saying
that the concern wasn't there. I don't want to judge anybody, or
second-guess anybody's intentions. I'm only saying that I
personally could never see anything more than a political intent
in this sort of talk.

"And then, yes, we were told to quit our posts. We were told
to quit them because there were 'too few priests.' When I was
teaching philosophy at the national university there were even
fewer, at least I think there were fewer, but nobody ever
complained that I didn't have an assignment in a parish or some
other fixed pastoral work. And I never knew of anyone, not one
bishop, concerned over the fact that there were priests in our
school who taught mathematics or English or history or Spanish
all day. I really had to wonder why all this concern all of a
sudden! It seemed to me that teaching our people to read,
teaching the poor, the illiterate, was more important to the
church's mission than being in the university, teaching the
privileged, teaching them subjects such as the ones I'd taught
there.

"I knew that other countries had priests in government
positions—important positions—and no problem was ever made

of it. To come down to cases, I was in Colombia a few days ago, and a fellow Jesuit was telling me he'd been working in the ministry of education and had never had a problem. So, then, is it all right to have a job in a government ministry in Colombia but not all right in Nicaragua?''

"It hurt, and it still hurts, not to be able to celebrate Mass. But I accepted. I thought of Charles de Foucauld."

''I have to say that it really hurt to accept the conditions the bishops laid down for granting us permission to keep our government positions in July 1981. An agreement like that looked really absurd to me, because we were being given permission to keep the posts we held, as an 'exception,' in view of the emergency situation in the country, but we were being asked voluntarily to give up all exercise of our priesthood. Now we could no longer celebrate any sacrament, not even the Eucharist, in public or private, in Nicaragua or anywhere else. But it was 'voluntary,' so that it couldn't be interpreted as a punishment.

''This doesn't seem to me to be either canonical or pastoral or evangelical or Christian or human. If the concern is pastoral, if what's wanted is for us to go back to the pastoral ministry, the kind of deprivation that's asked of us takes us still further out of the pastoral ministry. For over a year now we've been deprived of every kind of directly pastoral and priestly ministry. We've kept the commitment we made, but there's no way we wouldn't feel the deprivation as a penalty, and suffer from it as such—feel we're being punished by being deprived of something. And if we've committed no crime (after all, we're being permitted to keep our jobs), then why are we asked voluntarily to accept—that is, voluntarily to impose upon ourselves—a penalty? The agreement says it's not a penalty, it's a voluntary renunciation. But it's *felt* as a penalty; there's no way for it not to be felt as one.

''I believe that if there's an exception to be made by the Church here—if the church is willing to make this exception, out of consideration for an emergency in the life of the people—then this exception ought to be made generously. The priests ought to have the church's blessing and support, so that they wouldn't lose the spirit of the priesthood, and so that they wouldn't turn away, not lose the taste for the sacramental ministry and become unaccustomed to this ministry, while they're devoting themselves to this exceptional work. If the church has their spiritual good at heart and grants this exception, it should find a way to help them pastorally and spiritually while doing so.

"For instance, there was a bishop who got us together and told us, 'I want to make a monthly retreat with you, so you can continue to reflect on your faith and keep the call of your priesthood alive.' This, it seems to me, is the way to make a pastoral response to our pastoral problem. Hasn't the church always insisted that all priests, even those who for various reasons don't preside at a community Mass, ought to be able to celebrate Mass themselves, even if with a minimal congregation?

"It hurt to be deprived of this, and it still hurts. But I accepted, voluntarily. I thought of Charles de Foucauld. I'd read that, because canon law in those days forbade the Eucharist to be celebrated without an acolyte, and he was with the Tuaregs in the Sahara and didn't have anybody to serve his Mass, he went three years without saying Mass so he could serve the Tuaregs by the witness of his evangelical presence. So I decided I could give up saying Mass in that same spirit. I said to myself, I'm going to give up celebrating all sacraments or performing any priestly function in order to be of service to my people by my presence in their revolution.

"Of course, Charles de Foucauld was completely alone and had to give up Mass altogether. I, thank God, don't have to give it up: I assist at the Eucharist celebrated by my confreres in my religious community.

"Along with these considerations, I ought also to mention a deep, unexpected satisfaction I have in certain things. We get a lot of letters from a great number of countries in America and Europe—from Christians, priests, theologians, basic communities, Christian congresses and assemblies, and so on. One very special one came from the whole editorial board of *Concilium,* which was meeting in London at the same time we were winding up our negotiations with the bishops. More than twenty world-famous theologians wrote to our bishops about how valuable they thought our presence and work were in the revolution. That made us realize how much our presence in the Sandinista revolution meant as a sign, in many lands—a clear sign of a church in solidarity with the cause of the poor.

"Nicaraguans were begging for this sign to be kept alive; they were saying that our presence in the revolution meant hope for them, as church. It was such a consolation for us to receive all this support. And in Nicaragua too there were so many documents, statements, assemblies, and meetings expressing a desire that we continue as priests *and* continue working for the people in the revolution."

> *"Any step taken against a commitment to the people would be against God's will. It would be a sin."*

"One hears it said that now you practice 'Jesuit obedience' to the Sandinista Front—that you obey the party blindly, whereas you disobey the authority of the church."

"In the first place, let's be clear about one thing. The other priests—the cabinet ministers—and I have remained in our offices with the permission of our bishops. This was arranged by none other than the Vatican secretary of state, Archbishop Casaroli. He played an important part in the agreement that had already been reached in Rome when the bishops called us together in July 1981 to give us this exceptional permission, under the conditions we've already talked about. We're not being disobedient. Let's be clear about that.

"To say we obey the party blindly seems rather coarse to me. But we had better talk about it. I don't believe there's anybody in the party, priest or not, with any self-respect or enjoying the respect of others, who could be said to be practicing blind obedience. Nobody. And least of all we.

"One of the fundamental principles of the party is 'democratic centralism'; we can certainly always have a hearing.

I can state publicly that, on numerous occasions, I have communicated directly with the leaders of the revolution, to ask them questions or to transmit my reservations or my suggestions, and that I continue to do so. Any sort of 'blind obedience,' in the pejorative sense, is foreign to everything I stand for. I have never practiced it, not even in the religious life—and nobody normal practices it, because it's beneath human dignity. Still less would it be an act of religion or a Christian practice. Those who know us know that we've always been very independent persons; we say what we think.

"But there is something more complex and deeper here. I feel very deeply the religious call to obedience to God. Never in my life have I made greater sacrifices out of obedience to God than in the revolution. And never, in my thirty years of religious life, have I understood more profoundly the importance of 'obedience in faith,' which is obedience to the will of God. I hear this call of obedience to God in the voices and cries of our people suffering in poverty. I seek to obey God more than anything else on the face of this earth, and I feel that no one, nothing, can separate me from the path of obedience. And I can say without exaggeration (and without vanity—we've had enough training in risking our lives) that I'm not afraid even of death. I'm not afraid. I'm ready to do anything to be obedient to my conscience. And my conscience tells me to obey God by being unconditionally faithful, always, every moment, to my people—to a people still suffering in a country where three years is too short a time for the miracle of a passage from misery to development, where there are so many needs, where there is such a heritage of pillage and destruction, where there's been a blockade, where we're under attack. . . .

"I'd like to make it very clear that, by my faith in our Lord and my obedience in faith to our Lord to whom I've consecrated myself in the religious life and the priesthood, my conscience obliges me, after considering everything involved, to make this irreducible, irrevocable, irreversible commitment to the people. And for me it's clear that this is what God asks of me, that this is what God wishes. And I'm ready to obey his will even if it leads to my death. And there's nothing, there's no one, that can make me abandon it. For me, anything else, anything against a commitment to the people, goes clearly against the will of God and would be a sin.

"I've had very striking personal experiences in which I've seen that I'd be betraying God, and failing in the accomplishment of his will, if, in the name of some 'law' or other, I were to abandon my people—the poor in Medellín, or the students who went on a hunger strike for their comrades who were being abused by Somoza's National Guard. And I feel the same thing now. Only, I feel it much more profoundly, because that was just the beginning."

> *"I fear the risks of power. I strive to place everything I have in the service of the poor."*

"There are those who accuse you priests of holding these official positions in the revolution out of vanity, out of ambition for glory and power, or out of self-interest and personal advantage."

"Faced with this type of accusation there's no point in grandiloquent declarations of humility and unselfishness. Let's look at the facts.

"The pay in this revolution is low. With the training we've had, we could earn lots more, anywhere, doing anything. This country, and the Sandinista Front, have tremendous economic difficulties. When I was working in the national Crusade for Literacy I made the highest salary in government—10,000 cordobas a month, $200 to $300 at the official exchange rate. Now that I'm working with the youth movement I make 3,000 cordobas—$100—a month. If I'd accepted the position of vice-minister, I'd still be making 10,000 cordobas. There's no social security for us. Money is the least important thing.

"When they talk about glory and power, I don't know if they realize that this is a revolution that's being hounded relentlessly, fenced in, by imperialist administration hawks in North America, who make no secret of their 'covert' operations geared to the destruction of the revolution—which means destroying us, too. We could be murdered. This imperialism maintains, protects, feeds, and arms six thousand Somozist gunmen, just across the border in Honduras. And they make border raids, they attack and kill peasants and militia personnel. At any moment they could cross the border in a body, as the spearhead of an invasion by the Honduran army, and with the North Americans right behind them.

"At best, the future holds twenty to twenty-five years of very hard work. Privation is going to be our daily bread. You're seeing it right now. In addition to all the other deprivations and difficulties our people have had to suffer, there are the floods we've had this year, with forty bridges washed out, the good soil swept away, and the general destruction that's set the economic recovery of the country back ten years. And after the floods there was the drought. Power, glory, and personal advantage? Anybody in contact with our objective reality knows that we're a revolution practicing a severe, obligatory austerity. No, the only thing the revolution has to offer us is sacrifice, and the only privilege it accords us is service to the people. There's no margin for 'power' or 'glory' or 'personal advantage.' This is factual, this is objective.

"Being a cabinet minister in an underdeveloped country is not the same thing as holding a post in the ruling party of a country where the per capita income is high and the gross national product is in the billions of dollars. We're a tiny little country, very poor, and very abused and battered. Our statistics are a laugh. And we have to reckon with the danger of death constantly. That's the danger you live in when you're directing a revolution that's threatened as lethally as ours is, a revolution that the CIA is working to destabilize—this has been admitted by officials high up in the Reagan administration. Everyone knows who we are, we live in ordinary homes, we have no secret service to protect us, we go home at night, and anybody could ride up on a bicycle and shoot us and ride quietly off. And the U.S. government has put $19 million into getting rid of this revolution.

"Power? I'd like to state very clearly that we don't have any power, we don't wield power. The power here is in the hands of the Sandinista Front, with nine persons in its national administration, and it's a power of the people, for the people.

It's not the party's and it's not for the party. We only share the work and the efforts being made to restore and rebuild the country. We give no orders, and we make no policy decisions. We serve, and that's all. We're respected and listened to, yes. But that's something else. This ought to inspire trust, not jealousy or envy or objectively baseless accusations. Because we just don't have any power. Anyone who talks about power, as if we priests in the government and the party had any, simply doesn't know this revolution.

"I'm a member of the Sandinista Assembly, which is the advisory committee of the national administration of the revolution, and there's not one privilege attached to this job. But I wanted to explain this thing about power more clearly to you, since, to be sure, we're in a revolution that has 'come to power' and, in spite of all the limitations of our country, has access to power. For me, what's basic, what's evangelical, here lies in two attitudes, which I strive at all times firmly to maintain: my fear of the dangers of power, and my strong resolve to place power, to the last particle, exclusively at the service of the poor."

"I don't have to 'give my blessing' to the revolution. It's legitimacy rests in its consistency with the gospel."

"Another accusation I've heard against you: You're priests, yet you're partisan. You sacralize, you legitimate a revolution and a regime that, according to its accusers, brings communism and atheism to Nicaragua."

"Once again I have to say that this is an objection that doesn't correspond to reality here. It looks like a prefabricated accusation, invented by one ideology against another ideology. It's politically self-serving.

"I don't know if this accusation would be valid in some other country where priests occupy public positions, but it certainly doesn't hit home in Nicaragua. It doesn't correspond to the truth of our real situation.

"If they're thinking of Nicaragua as a stabilized, developed, tranquil country, where a number of political parties are struggling for power and a priest joins one of these parties and takes political sides so as to 'come to power,' and not to serve the people—then they're thinking of something quite different from what's happening here.

"To go back for a moment to the beginning of this interview: I came here to a country that'd been governed for nearly half a century by an unjust, murderous, bloody dictatorship, one that eradicated whole families. I read to the U.S. Congress whole lists of families—father, mother, grandparents, teenagers, and younger children—murdered in the mountains. In the final fifty-two days of the offensive alone, fifty thousand persons died in Nicaragua. Here, then, taking sides with the people by joining with those who are struggling and offering their lives to defend the people—supporting them and becoming one of them, in the people's defense—this is totally different from the case of political parties that are all trying to come to power in a normalized, organized country.

"We're taking sides, yes—with the good Samaritan. Here you have to take sides, you have to be 'partisan.' Either you're with the slaughtered or you're with the slaughterers. From a gospel point of view I don't think there was any other legitimate option we could have made. What is transpiring here in Nicaragua is rife with 'exceptionality,' and this exceptionality surely justifies our offices and our labors.

"As to the support, legitimation, or 'sacralization' we're accused of lending this revolution and its ideology by our priesthood—well, the truth is we've always been cautious in the extreme. We've always been most careful not to utilize our faith and our priesthood as a tool to this end. For us, and for anybody who's honest and objective, this revolution is legitimate in its own right. It doesn't need a priest to come and 'give his blessing.' Its legitimacy, stemming from the search for justice and liberation of the exploited, is such that a Christianity and a church that are faithful to the gospel and not manipulated can have nothing against this revolution and nothing to fear from it. Quite the contrary, such a Christianity and such a church must see that this revolution is humanely and socially legitimated in virtue of its consistency with the gospel, because it liberates our poor, outraged, exploited, Christian people.

"But the extreme right utilizes and manipulates Christianity and the church, in order to attack the revolution and deprive it of its legitimacy—in order to make it look suspect, communistic, and atheistic, a persecutor of the faith and the church. This confuses our simple, religious-minded people. And this is how the ultraright gets the church outside Nicaragua, especially in Rome, through the Latin American Bishops' Conference, to take sides against the revolution. And they rely on the efforts of the Reagan administration to destabilize us. It's this manipulation that's at the origin of the accusation you're reporting."

"I've lived with lay persons and I've lived with religious, and for ten years now I've lived with members of the Sandinista Front. And I really have to wonder—where are all the atheists?"

"This accusation of communism and atheism is an interesting one. I think that most persons who talk that way about Marxism are resorting to a caricature—an insulting caricature. They're coming from an ideological, political, self-serving, anti-communist stereotype that distorts Marxism because they haven't the courage to look at it for what it really is. It's one thing when someone undertakes seriously and scientifically to see what Marxism really is, and what is really Marxist here in our revolution—what the Marxist approach to the social sciences has contributed to the building of this revolution. But it's a different thing altogether when accusers not only don't know what Marxism is, but distort it and use a caricature of it to denigrate, to cheapen, and to malign, effortlessly and underhandedly, anything that's done for the poor.

"Let them be serious, respectful, and objective for once. Let them take the trouble to analyze each ideology in its own turn, and then analyze what there is, and what there isn't, of each ideology here in our revolution. Let them not simply resort to empty epithets. Let them look at our history, our reality, and what this revolution really is and is doing.

"We're surrounded by a great chorus of anticommunists, incited by the anticommunist political hawks in the present U.S. imperialist administration. They think they can profit from name-calling, if they manage to convince others that their caricatures really do point to a false, evil force. But this shows only that those who use this dirty ideological weapon in Nicaragua are making illegitimate and dishonorable accusations.

"Atheism? I grew up in a Jesuit boarding school in Nicaragua. Then I spent thirty years in religious houses. And now, over the last ten years, I've been working in intimate contact with fellow members of the Sandinista Front. And I really have to wonder—where are Nicaragua's atheists?

"I'm convinced that the biblical concept of the atheist is the correct one. In the Bible, the atheist is the one who doesn't love. That's who really denies God. I have comrades who say that they 'don't believe,' that they 'don't have the faith.' But they've been living a life of love, a life of commitment—they've given the gift of self and of sacrifice—for twenty years now in the cause of the poor. Certainly this will be acknowledged on the Last Day as genuine faith. And I know others who, in the name of God, are slitting peasants' throats out on our borders, to create panic.

"There are ladies and gentlemen in our country who, with the name of God on their lips, have stopped making investments here so that there will be an economic crisis in Nicaragua. They are sending their money out of the country because they say this revolution is Marxist and atheistic. They are attacking their own people in the name of God. There are those who, in the name of God, think themselves summoned to be a dominant class. They convince themselves that God has chosen them to be superior to others, so that of course others should serve them. This is their faith. And this is their God, whittled down to the level of their privileges and interests.

"Who in Nicaragua really believes in God? And who really are the atheists in Nicaragua? If these questions are asked in all sincerity, the answers are obvious.

"Admittedly, I've been talking about extreme cases. Between the extremes come the sincere, explicit believers who constitute the vast majority of our people, and of course they are true believers in God. But if I had to choose between the extremes—and of course I have to!—I prefer to be with those who, without putting God's name on their lips, and perhaps without even formally knowing God, are doing all God asks to be done for a suffering people. They carry God's love, yes, and God's tenderness, in their hands and in their lives."

> *"The basic motivation for all I've been doing for over thirty years is Christ."*

"Have you traded in the gospel for Marx? Have you turned your back on Christ to practice the 'following of Marx'?"

"I can state categorically that I have not exchanged, am not exchanging, and shall never exchange Christ and the gospel for anything or anyone else. For me, Christ and his gospel have been for over thirty years the basic motivation of my life, and of everything I've done and am doing. And it's my life goal to live and die according to the model that Jesus has taught us in the gospel.

"This question—this accusation—wouldn't deserve an answer at all if it weren't for the fact that we can't afford to leave any doubt about our personal attitudes. We have to 'give an account of our hope,' state the reasons why we hope for the things we hope for. But taken in itself the objection is absurd, because it tries to compare apples and oranges. Christ and Marx aren't on the same level; they don't fall in the same category of things at all.

"The basic motivation of my life and work is evangelical. This is the motive power, the moving force of my life, the fundamental motivation that leads me to work for the upbuilding of the kingdom of God here on earth. But the gospel contains no manuals of architecture, engineering, or social science to help us in the practical building up of this new society, which the kingdom of God obliges us to build. As Vatican II clearly states, the kingdom of God begins to be built in concrete history. So we have to have recourse to all the sciences that can help us: philosophy, physics, chemistry, engineering, the social sciences—and among the social sciences, Marxism.

"The only thing we look for in these sciences is what's appropriate for our own situation. We use them only to help us solve the concrete problems we have to face in building a new Nicaraguan society. And I'm trying to help form this society, one that's in line with my basic motivation, the gospel of Jesus Christ.

"Jesus with his gospel and Marx with his socio-economic critique are two different sorts of things. I don't think it would make any sense for someone to say he or she is exchanging Christ for Galileo, or Newton, or Einstein, or some famous chemist, would it? Well, Marx is on the same level as they, and it doesn't make sense to say he can be exchanged for Christ. We don't exchange Christ for anything or anybody else."

> *"I think that in Nicaragua the ministry of charity and love is being translated into a ministry in support of the forward march of the people."*

"Here's another accusation for you—a challenge really: some are saying that you ought to define, once and for all, whether you're priests or whether you're politicians."

"We've already defined ourselves. We've been defining ourselves for years. We've always spoken and acted as Christians, priests, and persons of faith, committed to our people's struggle, by the power of the gospel and for the sake of the gospel.

"Our service of God in the priesthood has led us to the ministry of charity and love, which in Nicaragua has been translated into a ministry in support of the forward march of the people, the ministry of accompanying our people from within, by participating in a transformation of structures, so that the poor may have justice. Our first definition, then, our essential definition, must include, because of the concrete historical exigencies of the ministry of charity, the element of support for the Sandinista popular revolution.

"I don't think we need any more 'definitions' in order to be well defined. But I'm ready to give one if it's insisted on, at any time, and I'll give it right now: I'm a Christian, I'm a priest—I seek to live in such a way as always to be faithful to God, faithful to the church, faithful to the priesthood, and faithful to God's grace. And in order to live out these fidelities concretely, historically, among my people, I have no thought or desire ever to betray my people, their history, or their revolution.

"If we study the defense of the cause of the poor with the eyes of faith, we find God deep within it. In defending the cause of the poor we're defending God's cause. God's cause is transcendent, this is true. But it includes all the positive causes of history, and preferentially the cause of the poor, for God has caught them up in history in a preferential option. We believe we can reach God in Nicaragua only through the mediation of the struggle for and with the poor.

"I think that those who are asking us to 'define ourselves' are asking us to put asunder something that we feel God has joined together here in Nicaragua. What they want is for us to either abandon the priesthood or abandon the popular revolution— two things that I feel to be profoundly united in my life, in my faith, and in my spirituality. I feel, profoundly, that I am a priest, and at the same time I feel, profoundly, that I am committed to the cause of our revolution. For me, the suggestion that we keep these two things apart is as absurd as asking a French Christian to make up his or her mind to be either Christian or French, or asking a Spanish Christian to define whether he or she is a Christian or a Spaniard. It's ridiculous to ask someone to choose between two things that can go together perfectly well."

> *"My work with the Sandinista Front has shown me how to live the gospel more realistically."*

"Your political activity, your fight for the people, your labors in the revolution, with the Sandinista Front—what effect has all this had on your faith and your spiritual life?"

"From the very beginning, I found that my part in the Sandinista struggle gave me the opportunity to live the gospel more realistically. I was now living that gospel in a basic, radical way—a way that was not just theoretical, not simply a matter of doctrinal formulas, and not expressed only sporadically in writings or in isolated actions of daring. I was now living the gospel in my whole practical life. The Sandinista Front provided me with the opportunity of daily risking my life for the cause of the poor—flesh-and-blood persons I see and esteem, the ones I've opted for on criteria that are sacred, religious, and Christian—the criteria of the gospel—out of a desire to follow Christ and be Christ's priest as he was the priest of his Father and risked his life for these same persons, and actually died for them.

"The Sandinista Front gave me the chance to have what we used to pray for in the novitiate—flooded with the fervor of the moment and perhaps not completely realizing what we were asking for—'the grace of martyrdom, if it were to be God's will.' Now that request is concretized for us in our lives, day and night, as we stand ready to lay down our lives for the people. Under Somoza the risk of going to prison, of being tortured and murdered, was a reality that, alas, thousands of Nicaraguans had to face. And the nightmare has not ended with the triumph of the revolution. Counter-revolutionaries have already begun to murder technicians and Sandinistas. In 1982 they killed more than five hundred Nicaraguans, and the attacks grow more vicious by the day.

"I must add that I've found countless examples of heroism among my fellow revolutionaries—examples of high-mindedness, of selflessness—in their dedication of love to our people, to the lowliest of our people. Theirs is a practical love, which has renewed in me all those evangelical and religious attitudes that I had been trying to live for years and years, but they had become routine, locked up in the patterns and limits of our routine religious life. Some religious end up identifying the experience of the evangelical virtues with these patterns, these surroundings, these limits; they think that the evangelical life can't be lived outside these molds.

"In our Latin American countries this can actually snuff out the evangelical life, a life according to the gospel, for our men

and women religious. Here we are, living in community, all
leading a correct, 'observant' life—but it's the life normally
lived by religious in normal times in a normal country. Not that
my community isn't a fine community from the religious point
of view. I've never had problems with my community, and I've
never left it, except for the months when I had to go into hiding.
And I live, I share, I pray, and I nourish my faith in this
community. Nevertheless, I gained a new dimension, new
religious vitality, when I started sharing my life with my fellow
Sandinists—the heroic dimension, I'd call it.

"I had lived in community with other religious who had made
a commitment that, from the ascetic viewpoint, was a holocaust.
That's the kind of renunciation it demands. And yet, after so
many years, that way of life actually became simply normal for
us. Then, with my fellow Sandinistas, as I shared my life with
them—as I shared their experiences—I discovered a boundless
field where love and dedication could have free rein, where the
possibilities for toil and sacrifice for others were endless. This
was so motivating for me! It renewed me within.

"It was much more fruitful than any kind of spiritual
exercises or retreats to see the example of my fellow Sandinistas,
men and women, girls and boys, going to their death with such
courage, and with no wish but to fight to the death rather than
place their fellow Sandinistas in danger. And fight to the death
they did, and sometimes it was death by torture. For this cause,
for love of their people, these young persons steadfastly endured
the most atrocious tortures. And life in hiding was fraught with
danger and enormous sacrifices. All this was a great inspiration
for me, and has been truly precious for me, for my faith and my
religious life."

> *"Fidelity to my people in their
> battle has always been a
> powerful reason for being
> faithful to my vow of
> celibacy."*

"I must tell you too that this commitment of mine has given
me a new reason for and added a new meaning to my vow of
celibacy. Some of the reasons we were given in the novitiate for

looking on celibacy as supremely pleasing to God, a very special charism that God gave to the church, are no longer very good reasons. Not that they were false reasons then, but after thirty years of religious life and the great number of changes that renewal has wrought in the church, they're reasons that are no longer compelling. But this commitment to my people, as they make their difficult way along the path to total liberation and development, has given me a new and powerful reason for celibacy. That new reason lies in the importance of being faithful to the people, to the poor, and to the cause of the poor, for the sake of the kingdom of heaven.

"My celibacy radically expresses my profound, religious, transcendent involvement with the poor among my people. This reason—loyalty to my people in its struggle—has been a mighty reason for fidelity to celibacy. And it still is. Many a time it has been the most powerful reason of all for my being faithful to celibacy—in order to be faithful to my priesthood and thus to be able to place everything I have and am at the service of the cause of the poor. My priesthood, of course, is precisely one of the elements of my own personal contribution to the revolution.

"Without a doubt, we live on the borderline between faith and atheism, in some ways. We have close personal contact with persons who've never had the faith, or who've lost it—often enough owing to scandal occasioned by the church itself or positions taken by the church. We live on the frontier between the traditional atmosphere of a believer's religious life, the atmosphere in which many of us imbibed the faith in our earliest years, and close personal association with persons who either never had this faith or who don't talk about it because the atmosphere is not there, the right moment never comes. And living on this frontier makes you purify your own faith.

"I have to confess that my life of faith was always a very peaceful, tranquil experience. I was reared in a deeply Christian family. As a young boy I went off to a Jesuit boarding school, for six years, and then straight into the novitiate. I never had any real problems with my faith. My faith journey was a very calm one. And so when I joined the Sandinista Front, I leapt for the first time into an atmosphere where I was not surrounded by visual, audible, or ritual expressions of the faith. I crashed into unexpected questions concerning my faith. But this is not a bad thing. It hasn't done me the least harm. On the contrary, my faith has solidified; it's no longer a faith with a good percentage on loan from others, so to speak.

"In the midst of all this new self-questioning, then, and these new difficulties—but also amid countless examples of heroic love and sacrifice, even of the sacrifice of the gift of life itself—I've gradually made my faith more my own. It's more a part of me now, stronger, deeper.

"There are a lot more things I could tell you. But I'd like to just capsulize them, in a simple statement of what my experience has been.

"I'm about to complete ten years as a member of the Sandinista Front. And I can tell you two things. First, I have never, in all the years of my involvement with the FSLN, encountered the least obstacle to my faith or my morals. I have never had to make a decision, or do anything else, that placed my faith or my morals in danger or caused any problem for them. Second, what I found instead was a powerful stimulus to be a better Christian—to be more faithful to my Christian sensibilities, to live the real values of the gospel that my religious consecration calls for in a better and deeper way, and with more enthusiasm, both at the level of a deeper doctrinal grasp of these values and at the practical level of actually living them."

> *"A good many Christian students are in the Sandinista Youth Movement. Some are in its leadership."*

"Fernando, what does the provisional nature of your political duties mean to you, if anything? Do you still think of these duties as 'exceptional'?"

"I certainly do. In this country, in this revolution, which is so dynamic and so dialectical, nobody can feel permanently ensconced in a position, wedded to a job.

"But I'd like to go into this further. The assignment is provisional, yes. But my commitment to the people is not. My involvement in this revolutionary process has nothing provisional about it whatsoever. It's definitive. It's a lifelong,

total commitment for me, just as are those other commitments
I've made and expressed in faith in the gospel, in Christ, and in
God. It's for the gospel, Christ, and God that I've made this
commitment and it's for them that I live. It will never be
legitimate for me to doubt that this commitment is to be
honored out of loyalty to the faith itself, out of the following of
Jesus Christ. There's nothing provisional here. This is a decision
to the death.

"I do not, however, suppose that I am the only one who could
fill this position. I think I make a contribution to it. My fellow
Sandinists consider my presence in this post beneficial. I'm
accepted by the rank and file, the grassroots. But I can be
replaced. I don't have the top position in the Sandinista Youth
Movement. I'm a national vice-coordinator. There's a national
coordinator, and he's the real dynamo of the Sandinista Youth
Movement, its driving force."

*"If you resigned, which do you think would stand to lose more,
the revolution or the church?"*

"This revolution is poor. Its resources are scant. Every leader
and every follower is important, necessary. In this sense, the
relinquishing of any position in the revolution would represent a
loss for the revolution, especially if it entailed leaving the
revolution itself. Ten thousand technically-trained persons have
left Nicaragua. Anyone who's studied in the university or has
had an academic training like mine is important in this country,
and so of course my resignation would be a loss to the
revolution.

"But it would also be a loss to the church. In Nicaragua there
has been a positive integration of Christians in the popular
revolution. This is precious for the church. It's the first
revolution in the history of the human race that Christians have
been this deeply and this positively involved in. If any of us left
the revolution, I would consider it a loss for the church, because
the church would lose its presence in the revolution. If the
church doesn't want the revolution to be atheistic, and
atheizing, then the first thing it should do is to be present in it as
God's witness. If the church pulls Christians out of the
revolution, it will be cooperating in the 'atheization' of the

revolution: the revolution will become atheistic and it will make atheists of others.

"I doubt if there has ever been another revolutionary party or revolution anywhere in the world that's entrusted the responsibility for the political formation of its youth—its future as a revolution—to a Catholic priest. But Nicaragua did it. The church has always been most zealous for the education of youth, has it not? So, then, ought it not to see my presence in the Sandinista Youth Movement as a guarantee of, and an advantage for, its educational mission?

"I don't understand how the same ones who complain that Christians aren't allowed to join the Communist Party of Cuba then turn around and complain that the Sandinista Party in Nicaragua not only allows Christians to join it but appoints them members of the Sandinista Assembly and entrusts the political directioning of its youth movement to a priest! This ought to be seen as something positive. It ought to be recognized that if this were to be lost, the church would suffer a loss. I could be replaced, of course, but my replacement might be someone who, by training and experience, would have no appreciation of the Christian faith or the church."

"Are there any Christians in the Sandinista Youth Movement?"

"Of course! If this revolution has any special characteristics of its own, the very first is the integration of Christians—many, many Christians, at every structural level. The Sandinista youth are no exception. A great many Christian students are active members, and there are Christians among the leaders.

"When the second national assembly of the Sandinista Youth Movement was in preparation, in December 1981, I invited some of the members of a group of Christian university students we have here in Nicaragua—the Revolutionary Christian Students —to come and talk. My intention was to invite them to the assembly as observers. But in the course of our conversation I realized that there wouldn't be any point in inviting them: they were already scheduled to attend, as active members of the Sandinista Youth Movement, and already elected as delegates to the assembly!

"The statutes of the Sandinista Youth Movement stipulate

that candidacy for membership is open to all youth without exception, and we keep to this.''

> *"I used to be afraid of torture. But now I'm not—though I know that when death comes, I'll be afraid. "*

"I'm going to ask you a blunt, personal question, Fernando. Are you at peace? Or are you anxious, or bitter, or sad?"

''I'm deeply at peace. I was at peace before the victory, in the midst of the struggle, and I'm at peace now. My sense of peace is very great, because I feel linked, with my whole being, to a great cause, a holy cause. I feel peace in the unification of my faith in God with this cause of the poor—which is the cause of Christ, because they're his own, the ones he loves most. This cause is the cause of the kingdom of God, and I have the peace of God within me.

''I feel so much at peace that nothing, no one, will be able to take it from me. I'm not afraid of anything that may happen in the future, whatever may come.''

"Aren't you afraid of death?"

''I think everybody's afraid to die—when the moment actually comes. Every time I've been in danger of death I've felt fear: concrete, physical fear. Whenever I was in danger of death in the past, I always felt the physical effects of fear, right here in my stomach. But little by little, as I worked with the Sandinista Front, I learned to look at death as a real possibility, every day, and I learned never to retreat from any commitment I'd made, even though I knew death might be waiting for me right around the corner.

''I can tell you this: I'm not afraid to face death, even though I know that when the moment comes I'm going to feel a natural, impulsive fear. But I won't retreat, any more than I ever retreated during the struggle against Somoza's military dictatorship.

''In the past, I was always afraid of torture. It was never a

fear that prevented me from doing my duty, though. We lived a
great part of the time in situations where the risk of torture and
death was a daily possibility. The best of us—the greatest, the
ones who've been the examples, the most admired and the most
courageous—have given their lives for this cause. And that's
where I learned that, for this cause, it's well worth laying down
your life."

> *"I pray every day of my life.
> I've made my most important
> decisions during prayer."*

"When do you pray, Fernando? And how do you pray?"

"Well, I see you want to strip me naked.

"I was never much for long prayers. I remember that when I
was in the novitiate the first day we prayed I was so distracted
that I asked a friend, someone I'd known in school, whether
he'd had any distractions himself. Only one, he said—from the
beginning of the hour right to the end. So it had been the same
for him, too!

"After all those years when we used to have silent prayer for
an hour, or an hour and a half, I came to the conclusion that I
don't have the contemplative charism, as my brother Ernesto
has, for instance. What I do have is a great facility for finding
God very quickly in prayer. I pray very frequently during the
day.

"I pray every day of my life, and I'd have to say that all the
most important decisions of my life have been made in prayer.
I've always lived my life with a sense of dependence on the
Lord—the clear consciousness that I'm a sinner, and need God's
grace and help. But I'm no longer afraid of God—which I was,
very much, in my first years in the religious life.

"I'll let you in on a little detail. Classical music always helps
me pray. I blend the music together with the prayer and express
myself to the Lord from right inside the music—trying to offer
God, in my being and in my life, something as beautiful as the
music. I always take a little tape recorder along in the car and
take advantage of the time these trips use up to spend some extra
moments in prayer this way. This is one of the ways I pray.

"In my community, where ten of us Jesuits live, we have our eucharistic celebration, and I usually participate. We have our monthly retreats, and I take part in them, too—we go on retreat Saturday and Sunday, out of town. Except when I was in hiding, and when I was living in political asylum in the Mexican embassy, I've always lived in a Jesuit community, wherever the provincial has assigned me. Community prayer is the most structured form of prayer I practice. My personal prayer is not so structured."

> *"I'm a priest forever. And I'm committed to this revolution to the death."*

"So many things can happen, Fernando, as far as priests in political office in the Nicaraguan revolution are concerned—how ready are you to obey the church if you're asked to do something very difficult?"

"I've meditated on this for some time, especially recently. I intend to keep my commitment to the church, and especially to the priesthood. Come what may—so many things can happen, things we can't foresee!—come what may, above all I want to stay in the priesthood. I feel a very deep ecclesial calling to work as a spiritual director. And whatever the circumstances, I intend to remain faithful to my priesthood—including celibacy, which is one of the clearest signs for our people that we're being faithful to our priestly vocation.

"If you'll permit me, I'd like to close this interview with a public declaration of my position regarding the priesthood. I'd like to recall the phrase I selected to appear beneath my name on the little 'holy card' I gave my friends on the occasion of my priestly ordination. It read *Fernando Cardenal, S.J., Sacerdote para siempre*—a priest forever. And today I want to reaffirm that 'priest forever.' I used to tell my brother Ernesto that nothing, no one, could take from us what we most love—our ideals, our priesthood. And so I say once more right now: I am a priest forever.

"At the same time, I have to restate all I've said concerning my commitment—to the death, if need be—to this revolution. I hope that no one will put asunder what God has joined together here in Nicaragua. In my case God has united my priesthood to the Sandinista popular revolution, which I love so much, and to which I feel committed with all the strength of my heart, with all my enthusiasm—and for this revolution I'm ready to shed the last drop of my blood.''

•

As Fernando finished, I was seated at the table in his office on the second floor of the July Nineteenth Sandinista Youth Building. It is a spacious office, with little furniture. There were some pictorial records of the national crusade for literacy on the walls. I saw portraits there, too—Eduardo Contreras, Carlos Fonseca, and Sandino. On his table, a multi-colored pennant proclaimed the Second Congress of Sandinista Youth, in Managua, December 19, 1982. There was a glass vase holding a green, leafy branch—sandalwood, perhaps.

The porch outside, and the walls of the meeting room, were one big mural—paintings, sketches, slogans, and faces of Sandinista youth fallen in combat. ''Our Heroes and Martyrs'' was the title. On my way out one of their slogans struck me. It stood in great letters on one of the walls: ''Let's not stop halfway—Carlos Fonseca.''

I walked out into the street, turned, and continued on my way, in the shade of the laurels. But that one sentence kept coming back to me. It fused in my mind with Fernando's own last declaration of fidelity: ''to the last drop of my blood.''

Students on the porch were getting their posters ready for a march. There was to be a funeral and protest march that afternoon, for the tragic death of seventy-five Miskito children in the Jinotega zone. The helicopter shuttling them out of reach of the Somozist bands across the Honduran border had crashed and burned. The mothers' weeping tore me to pieces. They were all less than five years old.

"I'm a priest—a missionary priest, essentially. I travel for the cause of peace, justice, and the dignity of my people."

Miguel d'Escoto, Foreign Minister

Miguel d'Escoto was born in Hollywood, California, on February 5, 1933. His parents were Nicaraguan, and shortly after he was born they returned with him to their native land. Miguel received his primary education in the La Salle institutes of Diriamba and Managua.

At the age of fourteen, he went to the United States, to attend Saint Mary's College, in Moraga, California, and Manhattan College, in New York City. He continued his studies in Latin and Greek in Scranton, Pennsylvania, and obtained his licentiate in philosophy in Glen Ellyn, Illinois. In 1956 he entered the novitiate of the Catholic Foreign Mission Society of America (Maryknoll), near Boston, Massachusetts.

He received degrees in theology (Maryknoll, New York) and education (New York State University), after studies lasting from 1957 to 1961. Upon completion of work in these two institutions he transferred to the Pulitzer Institute of Columbia University, New York City, for work in comparative journalism and political economics.

Miguel was ordained a priest in 1962, and in 1962 and 1963 served as assistant director of the Department of Social Communications of Maryknoll. In 1963 he went to Chile, where he worked in Santiago with the inner-city poor until 1969. There he founded the National Institute of Population Action and Social Research, with a view to improving the living conditions of the poor. This was an experience that marked his life permanently with the evangelical seal of dedication to the poorest of the poor. During these same years he made trips to

Brazil and Mexico, called there by church officials to evaluate pastoral work with the marginalized in the "misery zones" of both nations.

In 1970 he was appointed director of social communications of the Maryknoll Society, in New York. In this position, which he held until 1979, he had occasion to journey throughout Latin America, Europe, Africa, and parts of Asia, visiting Maryknoll missions. In 1979, in Nicaragua, he founded the Nicaraguan Foundation for Integral Community Development in León.

Beginning in 1975, when he first came in contact with the Sandinista National Liberation Front, he collaborated more and more closely with the anti-Somozist struggle, promoting solidarity committees in the United States.

In October 1977, in San José, Costa Rica, he joined the Group of Twelve, made up of fellow scholars and professionals committed to the struggle against Somoza through the FSLN.

With the triumph of the revolution, in July 1979, Father Miguel d'Escoto was named foreign minister.

Since September 1980, he has also been a member of the Sandinista Assembly.

•

I had doubted I could ever obtain an interview with d'Escoto. He was always away, it seemed, and when he was not, a chock-full agenda awaited him. There were always emergencies, for life in Nicaragua was beset with danger.

But Miguel returned from a long trip, and granted me a morning of peaceful conversation in his house—far from offices, secretaries, visits, and the phone.

I could have thought I was in a museum, and that the museum was in a park. Inside, there were paintings from every school of art and every land. In the garden, plants and flowers ringed the ranch-style house where we talked, and birds filled our ears with their song the whole time.

Miguel stretched out in a hammock, forgot his worries for a while, and spoke to me of his life, his faith, his weaknesses and temptations, his prayer, his pain, and his hope. He spoke with an intense concentration, and sense of detail, and transparency. The intonations in his sonorous voice revealed intimate nuances of sensitivity, sincerity, tenderness, and firmness. At times he seemed to be searching for just the right turn of phrase, and I guessed that he was translating from English to Spanish.

> *"This work offers me
> continual opportunities to
> speak of God in the way that a
> missionary priest ought to."*

"You've been named to a ministry that takes you on assignments of great urgency and responsibility, for Nicaragua's context today is certainly an unusual one," I said to him. "Don't you run into contradictions between the work of foreign minister and your priestly office? Do you manage to keep your priestly identity alive in the midst of all your trips and assignments? Surely they must be all-absorbing."

"You see, I can't even conceive a contradiction between being a Christian and being a decent human being, or between being a priest and being a responsible citizen. There can be no contradictions here. Being a Christian, and especially being a priest, obliges me to be a better citizen, a more responsible human being—more loving and respectful toward my brothers and sisters, more in solidarity with their battle for liberation from all the chains that keep them from living fully human lives and keep them in subjection to systems that blatantly contradict the will of God.

"The priest preaches Christ's message. He's a follower of Christ. But he ought to carry that message and preach it not only in words, but basically in deeds, in works—in works that make the words more understandable. Very often, no words of mine are necessary to make others ask, 'Why are you acting this way?'

"This is my experience today as a priest in government. I'm not the one who brings up the subject of religion, or Christ, or the gospel. I often find a cabinet minister, or other government official, or army officer, coming to my office to discuss some

brief matter and then saying—as if the idea had suddenly
dawned on him—'Look, I used to be kind of religious myself,
you know, . . . I went to Mass, I was interested in everything
about religion . . . but gradually I turned away. I considered the
church pretty irrelevant to the everyday questions I was so
involved with—things that the situation of our people showed
were so important. But now—certain things have started me
thinking. For example, why are you still in the priesthood? Why
did you become a priest?'

"I've learned that my colleagues here have little interest in
abstract theological questions. They have absolutely no interest
in such subjects. They're interested only in the 'why' of a given
action. They'd like to be able to understand why one has
dedicated one's life to the priesthood, religion, and the
church—for example, why, in spite of the contradictions
between what the gospel says and what some church-related
persons do, someone concerned about the real welfare of the
people still loves the church and says the church is important for
the people's quest for the integral transformation, conversion,
of society.

"Once a commandant in the revolution told me that
something was bothering him and he wanted to talk about it.
I'm not going to give his name, but it's someone everybody
knows. We were together one day, discussing something or
other, when he suddenly asked the others present to step outside
for a moment so that he and I could be alone.

" 'Look, Miguel,' he then said to me, 'I want to tell you
something: God is love.'

"That was it? That's what he wanted to tell me? Those were
his exact words. It was not a question; it was a statement: 'God
is love.'

"Then he said to me, 'God is infinitely powerful.'

"Another statement. But he finally came to his problem: 'If
God is love, compassion, mercy—and if God is almighty,
all-powerful—then why is there evil in the world? Why are there
sinners? Why do we hurt each other? Why are we permitted
to do this? Why do innocent victims have to suffer the
consequences of human malice?'

"The problem of evil, then. I found myself talking to him

about free choice, the need to be able to choose good freely, out of love. I gave him a series of traditional arguments you study even before theology, philosophical arguments, from theodicy, because this problem bothered the Greeks, the philosophers, too. So I gave him that type of argument. And he said, 'I don't like that. I don't like that answer. If that's the answer, then I think God's made a mistake.'

" 'God's made a mistake.' That's just the way he said it. 'God should have made everybody good, and free. Or those of us who would not be good, he should have made slaves to his own will.' This army officer would have wished us all slaves of the divine will so that innocent people wouldn't suffer.

"People don't say this sort of thing to just anyone. They say it only to one of their own, who is also a priest. The fact that you're a priest makes you the one they open up to when the right moment comes. We talked this way a lot during the war—all the time, all during the war. Others hardly ever call me 'Mr. Minister.' They always call me 'Miguel,' or 'Father.' Only in certain official circumstances do they ever call me 'Mr. Minister.' Even in other countries I am addressed as 'Father Miguel.' In fact, there are some countries where they just don't know what to call me, so they call me 'Comrade Father Minister'! That's what they call me in the Soviet Union —'Comrade Father Minister.'

"I don't see how there could be a contradiction between a priest's complementary services or ministries and his priesthood. In fact, as I've told you, in my work I'm forever running into opportunities to speak as a priest. And all this is much more appropriate to my case, because I'm not a parish priest, I'm a missionary priest, essentially a missionary priest. My mission is to provide a living witness to God's love—not per se among those who already have explicit faith in the Lord, but among those on the fence, or on the other side of the fence, who don't have this explicit faith, or don't have any faith at all. The missionary is a witness sent, not to help keep up the enthusiasm of those who have explicit faith, so that they may continue to give witness themselves, and let their light shine—but to be a witness in the darkness, where explicit faith doesn't shine.

"I've never worked in a parish in my life. But I never thought that meant I wasn't doing what I was supposed to be doing as a priest. I'm a missionary priest. And I've always felt fulfilled as a missionary; I've worked only where the light of faith was trying to pierce the darkness."

> *"I keep my self-identity as a priest because I already had very strong habits of prayer."*

"My previous missionary life prepared me marvelously well for my present service to my people. These long trips of mine, which take me away from home so often and for such long periods, didn't start with the victory of the revolution. Before I got involved in my people's struggle, I traveled a great deal more than I do now. As a missionary, I crisscrossed Africa, the whole of Asia, all of Europe, and all of Latin America, visiting all our missionaries as director of Maryknoll's Department of Social Communications. I founded and was the director of Orbis Books, and I traveled everywhere looking for authors whose thought was worth sharing with our mission-minded following in the United States. This is what I've kept doing in my present service.

"And I do it, not by just making trips—trips don't have any meaning in themselves—but by making trips for a cause, and by using my travels to strike up relationships with others you can share a cause with because it's the cause of peace, justice, and dignity for my people and all peoples, the cause I've committed myself to for Christ, as a Christian and as a missionary priest.

"Naturally, it's extremely difficult to maintain one's identity as a priest in the midst of the life I've had to start living—and not just for the last three and a half years either, but for five and a half years, because all this didn't just suddenly start the day we won. I was very active, all during the final struggle. It's extremely difficult, though, because the priestly identity calls for a life of prayer, a life of meditation and reflection on the word of God.

"Yes, it certainly is difficult. I suppose it must look practically impossible, because in my work there are tasks so tremendously pressureful that you don't really have so very much time to devote to formal prayer. Still, there are situations, and human tasks, to which history suddenly obliges you—to which God himself obliges you, so that carrying them out is part of fidelity to God. Suddenly you find yourself in these situations, and the Christian has to be able to accept them and overcome the difficulties they involve.

"In my case, I think that what helps me the most is that in my years as a priest, and in my missionary work all over the world, I already had very strong habits of prayer, had already had them for quite some time. I had already acquired the habit of praying any time, anywhere. Whether you're driving along in a car, or you're here in the office, or you're in the garden, you're praying, every moment. When I'm here, the garden is one of the places I find God most easily. That's why I like to go out in the garden. Often I'm out in the garden before five o'clock in the morning. Nobody talks to me when I'm out in the garden: they know I'm thinking, meditating, praying."

> *"I always felt sorry for those in misery. I was called a communist at the age of thirteen."*

"You say you began making your long trips more than twenty years ago, that your previous missionary life prepared you for this service to your people, and that you had very strong habits of prayer. What was your life like then? What experiences have molded you into the kind of person you are now? What brought you to what you're doing as minister of foreign affairs in the new Nicaragua?"

"First I have to say it was my family that made the decisive influence on me. My first memories here are from when I made my First Communion, before I went off to boarding school. I was five years old. I was supposed to make my First Communion only when I was seven. But my sister, who was six years old and taking catechism already, would come back and tell me everything. I liked this very, very much, and I asked permission to go and listen. And so I did, over facing the park, where the Assumptionist Sisters were, very close to where we lived at that time. Every time I go by there I remember. And when my sister finally went to make her First Communion, I begged and begged to be allowed to make it too. No, they told me, I had to be seven years old, and I was only five. Finally they decided to take me to the archbishop and let me try to convince him. I remember that day very well. My papa grabbed me and gave me a bath. I used to like to climb trees and chase after pigeons and peacocks, and go hacking down fruit off trees. And my papa told me, 'Now, you can't go to see the archbishop that way. I'm going to give you a good scrubbing, a good bath.' Then I went to see the archbishop, all nervous, in my short pants. And I made my First Communion when I was five years old.

"I would listen to sermons, even when I was a very young boy, and I would say I wanted to devote my life to saying those things and living that way. My sister and I would make plans. She was a little bigger, and she noticed something, and pointed it out to me: there were persons who didn't have anything to eat. So we talked the cook into making extra servings, then we would creep out of the house during siesta when everybody was asleep, and went looking for the little old ladies. Besides something to eat, we would give them sunflowers, or little blossoms with the Sacred Heart of Jesus on them. They lived under the grandstand in the National Stadium. The seats were wooden then, and they lived under them.

"And then my sister started talking to me about the pagans. I never quite understood—I thought the pagans were a particular race of people, I thought they were Chinese. My sister told me that we should 'give up dessert' to ask our Lord to send missionaries to the pagans, and convert the pagans. I often told her I'd 'offer up' dessert too, but while she was praying I'd gobble up both desserts. My father found out, though, and put an end to that.

"The Christian Brothers also had a great influence on me—in their school, their catechism classes, and so on. Everything I heard about religion, I related to what I saw and experienced. And I said it was simply not possible that there could be things such as I saw in the streets of Managua—people looking for something to eat in garbage cans. I used to pass the Terraza Club, where they had big garbage cans full of the leavings of banquets from the night before, and I would see people digging through them for something to eat. It hurt me very much to see this. But when I said anything about it, I was told not to worry, those people were used to it. And I said, 'Those people? They are the only ones there are!' This 'those people' business hit me like a sledge hammer. And that casual, calm way of accepting the misery of others as something normal—well, I just rebelled.

"At thirteen I was called a communist for the first time. And when I kept making remarks like this I kept being called a communist. I didn't know what a communist was, but it didn't seem to me it could be very bad, because it seemed to be someone who felt sorry for others when they were suffering, and that wasn't bad, that wasn't selfishness. So I'd answer ironically. For example, all the talk was about 'society' in Nicaragua in those days. I, supposedly, belonged to 'society.' That word made me sick! 'Right,' I would say, '*suciedad* ("dirt"). Oh, excuse me, I meant *sociedad* ("society").' That's how much I cared for 'society.'

"Around that same time, when I was thirteen, they were wondering at home whether it might be a good idea to send my sister and me abroad to study. The mother superior of Assumption School was Mother Francisca. She's still living, I love her very much, and have very nice memories of her, she's ninety-something now, but she's not there at the school any more, right near our house. Mother Francisca was going to Spain. A sister of my father was going with her, to enter the convent—Mother Amanda, who's here in Nicaragua, at La Palmera. My sister was going off to school with them, and papa said I should go to Spain to study too.

"But I didn't want to go to Spain. I'd heard there was a dictatorship there. We knew what a dictatorship was from Nicaragua. I was still quite young, but I was very much impressed by what I heard on the radio at night on the Voice of America. My papa used to listen to the news, and I was always hearing about continental solidarity and democracy. I thought solidarity and democracy must be something marvelous—I thought they must be talking about a society where persons would live more like brothers and sisters to one another. So I kept telling papa I didn't want to go to Spain; I wanted to go somewhere else to get ready to come back later and try to help make a different way of life, a better Nicaragua. Even then I had this restlessness. They paid attention to me when I talked like this, too. I was the oldest boy.

"When I was fourteen, I was finally allowed to go to the United States. We all went together, my sister, my parents, and I. My sister's plane left from the airport in New York, and we went to see her off. Then papa took me to California. And the only thing he told me, as he left me there, all alone, was never to forget my devotion to the Blessed Virgin Mary and to go to Mass every day. This was the only thing he told me to do, and I did it, every day. There's a strong tradition of devotion to the Blessed Virgin in my family. We always prayed the rosary together— papa, mama, the kids, and the persons who worked for us."

> *"I was an angry young man.*
> *I was angry at my country's*
> *predicament."*

"I'd been born in the United States. My father had quite a life story. When his father died, he was taken on as a page in the household of Archbishop Pereira y Castellón, in Managua. My father was a seminarian then. But he left the seminary, at the age of seventeen, and went to study in the U.S.A. He even acted in the movies. Then he met my mother. They got married, I came along, and they took me to Nicaragua. I was just over a year old. We got there just days after Sandino was killed, in 1934. My father entered the diplomatic corps under Somoza.

"But anyway, back in the United States, I began to live a lonely life, far from home. I was at Saint Mary's in Berkeley, which was a Christian Brothers school. I was an angry young man. I was angry at my country's predicament. I remember one time I was talking with Brother Edward, who was the dorm prefect. I was telling him about the situation in my country. And I told him, 'I hate the rich.'

"And Brother Edward said, 'I'm sure you don't hate them. You couldn't hate anybody.'

" 'What are you saying that for?,' I replied. 'I do too hate them!'

"And he asked me, 'Do you want something bad to happen to them? Do you wish evil on them?'

" 'I wish they wouldn't be the way they are.'

" 'Ah, then you're using the wrong word. You don't hate them.'

"This made me realize that what I really wanted was for the rich to change, not that something bad would happen to them. I just wanted those in misery to stop suffering, and I thought this would happen if the rich changed. I couldn't ever wish any evil on anybody.

"I didn't want to go back to Nicaragua for vacation. I stayed in the United States for the summer and went to work with immigrants who came there to work, without any English, and tried to make their living washing windows and jobs like that. In a world such as the one I saw around me, I related better to persons whose objectives were more like mine. I couldn't be with those who could talk only about whether they were going to Miami for vacation or somewhere else, or whether they were going out to the country club. I caught a kind of allergy to all those clubs and things.

"I remember one day I met a Nicaraguan, there in the United States, and after we'd talked a bit he said: 'So, Miguel, you haven't been back for three years? Then you're going to see how much nicer things are now. You'll see how things are changing.' I remember my heart actually started pounding within me.

" 'Really?' I asked. 'Tell me about it!' And he told me there was a new country club. What a disappointment. This was supposed to be something important, when it was for the benefit of only a handful of persons?"

> *"I wanted to be an engineer. I wanted to get married. But I kept being pursued by the thought that I had to do something to get ready to help change my country."*

"The day came when I had to decide what I was going to do with my life. I'd never lost the idea of doing something to serve my country. I remembered what I'd heard back in Nicaragua. We had big gardens around our house, with four full-time gardeners. It was like a park, and I liked to be with the gardeners. I would eat out there with them. My family were always telling me to let them alone, but I always went off with them. I liked to listen to what they talked about. I liked to hear about their problems. I loved to listen. There was one from the Atlantic Coast, and so I heard a lot about the coast. I had never been there, but he told how it was. He was a Miskito. And I heard about the problems of those who had a lot of children and not enough to support them. I was told that torrential rains would destroy their huts, and their problems would be compounded. And then, in California, in boarding school, I kept thinking of this situation. And I said to myself, I have to study for a profession that'll allow me to do something about problems like these. And I chose engineering.

"I might have chosen to be a priest. I'd had the idea since I was a boy. But at that stage, as a teenager in California, I was absolutely petrified at the idea. I wanted to get married. I wanted to have a family, I wanted to have children. I even had in mind the young woman I'd have liked to marry. So I went to college and studied engineering.

"But during my first year in college the idea of the priesthood began to come back into my head. It pursued me; I couldn't get away from it. I remember very well that one night a fellow student of mine, a Filipino, showed up in my room about ten o'clock. We were good friends. He wanted to go for hamburgers, or go to a dance, or something. I told him I couldn't because I was studying for exams. And he said to me, 'What're you studying all that for? You're not going to be an engineer. You're going to be a priest. Anybody can tell you're going to be a priest.' I got mad and talked to him for an hour about why I couldn't be a priest. I gave all the arguments. That really hit me, because I didn't want to be a priest.

"But the thought wouldn't leave me, and finally the day came when I couldn't sleep. Even when I went dancing, or went to parties—because I really loved to go to dances and spend my weekends partying and dancing—I couldn't get the thought out of my head that I ought to become a priest because that was the best way to help transform my country. There wasn't any Sandinista Front in those days, of course, or anything like it. I thought what had to be done was to change the direction of Nicaraguan society, and this couldn't be done by engineering. What was needed, I thought, was a conversion to a life of brothers and sisters, and this was what we ought to work for.

"Well, this idea kept pestering me, and I didn't like it. Finally I went to Brother Francis, who was in charge of us in the university there, and told him how this idea of being a priest was torturing me and I didn't like it. 'That's easy,' he said. 'Just say no. If you want to get rid of this idea, just say no. Unless you want to try it. Either try it, or say no.'

"But I couldn't say no. And I thought maybe God wants me to become a priest—then I can't say no. I might not like it, but I'm going to have to do it.

"I entered the seminary with the idea of always behaving in such a way that if I were sent away it wouldn't be my fault, it would be because my superiors judged that this wasn't the right path for me, this wasn't my vocation. I didn't go back to Nicaragua; I entered Maryknoll. I was scared to death of going back to Nicaragua. When I was eighteen or nineteen, and this business started coming into my head, I thought I just couldn't do it in Nicaragua. They'd stick me in the chancery, and I couldn't see that at all. I even said so to Archbishop González y Robleto, and he told me that if I thought I had to be one of those modern ones who had to go on horseback and be a missionary—well, that would be fine too. But I was afraid that in Nicaragua, because I belonged to a wealthy family and all that, I'd have distinctions and privileges I didn't want. I preferred to stay away, where I could just be the same as everybody else. This is what made me join Maryknoll. Then I saw that my love for my country had to expand, so that I was willing to go to any country at all as a missionary."

> *"From the day I became a missionary, I never thought, not for thirty seconds, of any possibility of ever leaving the priesthood."*

"I was never quite sure how much of a sacred obligation I might have to return home—to return to my country in need. I told my spiritual director about it, and he only told me to pray to resolve the doubt. But the doubt didn't go away. When it came time to take vows, the problem was there again. And I decided to put off making a decision until I was up for ordination to the diaconate. The feast of the Immaculate Conception was coming up. This is the big one for us. And I made a promise to the Blessed Virgin. I told her that on her feast day, December 8, I'd go to some priest who wasn't a friend of mine, somebody I didn't have any particular ties with, and ask him to give me an objective answer. I told her I'd ask him what I should do, and whatever he'd tell me, I'd do. I remember I wrote papa and mama and told them what I was going to do on December 8—that I was going to try to find the answer. And I asked them to pray for it to be the right one. I made a novena, and on December 8 I went to see Father Vincent Mallon. I told him everything, and he told me to stay put. I should stay where I was. And then and there I made up my mind. Period. I'm not one to go back and figure things out all over again. Once I've made a commitment I stick to it, and do it. And so I stayed in Maryknoll, and became a priest forever as a missionary. And never—not once in my life as a priest—have I ever wondered, even for thirty seconds, whether I ought to leave the priesthood. Not once.

"The most important thing in the seminary training was the novitiate year. The fact that Maryknoll had a novitiate was tremendously attractive to me, when I was thinking about entering. I wanted to have this opportunity, this luxury, this privilege, of being able to spend a period of time devoted totally to prayer and reflection. I had an excellent year. Excellent. So many of the things my spiritual director, my novice master, Father Charles Magsam, told us are still in me. One of the things he told us, which I fully understood only later, was: 'Don't be afraid to love.' Love was a risk, and commitment would bring suffering with it.

"When ordination time came, the most relevant thing in my life was a desire to do the will of God. It never occurred to me, for example, to suggest that I'd have liked to go to this mission, or that mission, even if I really would have liked to go there. No, I thought: it'd be nice if they'd send me to Japan, or Africa— but the best place to go will be the place they'll send me, because that'll be the will of God. I never experienced anything to make me doubt that.

"When assignment day came, I remember, there we were, standing in line, all thirty-six of us who were up for ordination, to go in and get our assignments. I was more or less in the middle of the roster: many had entered after college, and many had entered after studying Latin. I was terrible in Latin. I knew a lot of Greek, though. So I was pretty much in the middle of the list. And my classmates were all coming out with their mission assignments. 'Tanganyika!,' one would triumphantly announce (that was what Tanzania was called then). 'Japan!' 'Bolivia!'

"We bet on where we'd be sent. Everybody'd put in a nickel, and the one who had the most right guesses took the whole pot. What was bothering me was that everybody bet I'd be going to Rome for theology, and teach theology. I didn't look very kindly on this idea. I'd have liked to study theology—I'd have liked to go to Germany, though, probably because of Schmaus, Michael Schmaus (I'd read his eight-volume work, in Spanish, and had found it so interesting), and because of Karl Rahner, and other theologians I liked to read. I'd thought about this, but . . . well, I wanted to go to the missions. Then it was my turn. In I went—and to my great surprise, father general sent me to study comparative journalism in the Pulitzer Institute of Columbia University! I thought he must be kidding. But no, he was serious. And out the door I went, with the others saying, 'What's the matter with you?' I guess I looked pretty disappointed.

"But then I thought: it's the will of God. And I worked to be admitted to the Pulitzer Institute. It took work, too! Then I was assigned to Maryknoll itself, as assistant director of communications. And I did that for two years."

> *"In Chile, I lived with the poor. And I began to sense the presence of God in those who were the most downtrodden."*

"After two years I was sent to Chile. The only pastoral experience I'd had as a seminarian was four years helping out at Sing-Sing Prison, near Maryknoll, New York. It was a most interesting experience. I had a very good rapport with the prisoners. But I wanted to dress like them and live in the prison, so I'd be more their equal. I asked permission to do this, but I never got it.

"In Chile, I was asked to work at Bellarmine Center, and for a group called DESAL, *Desarrollo para América Latina* (Development for Latin America). Father Roger Vekemans had chosen priests from different parts of the world, but they were all Jesuits and I wasn't. Maryknoll let me work in DESAL, but I couldn't live at Bellarmine Center because I'd have been too cut off from my own congregation. I was sometimes referred to as a Jesuit. It still happens!

"So I went to Chile and started to work right away. They put me on a team that was studying inner-city slum life—the life of the *pobladores,* the slumdwellers of Santiago. The idea was not just to do research, but to get into contact with the grass roots, so the work wouldn't be just theoretical. I was offered several choices, and I chose CENAPO, *Central Nacional de Pobladores* (National Center for the Urban Poor), which I was already acquainted with—I'd once been invited to Chile by Lucho Quiroga, the founder, when I was on a trip to Venezuela and Argentina to meet with some union organizers. I was very interested in seeing how structures of union power could be hooked up with other organizational modalities—other structures that would be especially necessary in nonindustrialized countries, where union potential was so limited that they'd have to team up with other popular organizations to form a broad enough base.

"In CENAPO I got the idea of starting INAP, *Instituto de Acción Poblacional e Investigaciones* (Institute for Action and Research for the Urban Poor). It seemed to me that what was needed was not just an advisor, but many advisors, from all kinds of professions. So I founded INAP and gathered urban planners, physicians, attorneys, and others, for every kind of service to the popular organizations that were starting up among the inner-city poor, to defend workers and their right to organize.

"I dropped DESAL and devoted myself entirely to INAP. Now my life was the life of the *pobladores,* full-time. This was the beginning of a new stage in my spiritual and apostolic life.

"I remember some conversations I had around this time with the priest who'd been my novice master and spiritual director. He was in Chile too, in Concepción, and when he came to Santiago I took advantage of the opportunity to have some 'spiritual conferences' with him, some spiritual counseling. In one of these conferences I said to him, 'Father, I feel as if I don't really have faith.'

"I hadn't stated it very well, I guess, and he was surprised. 'What do you mean, You don't really have faith?'

" 'Well,' I said, 'I don't seem to *believe* in God now; I sense God, continually, and I see God, in human reality, with all its corruption, with all its shortcomings and problems. I see something wonderful, I see something much more human, much more humane, than what we have now. I see God's reflection in the people. And suddenly, I even notice things in me that aren't me. Suddenly I've noticed something like a spark from some fire that's not me.'

"This is what I meant by 'not having faith.' I'd begun to feel God as somebody so real, so close, in the people—even the derelicts, and prostitutes, and most 'destroyed,' you might say—that it was almost as if I didn't have to 'believe.' In the worst-off of all these human beings, I could glimpse the reflection of God.

"The time I spent in Chile—so completely immersed in the problems of the *pobladores,* and their search for a way out of them—was a big help to me in my spiritual formation. I was very happy there in Chile, doing that kind of work. Some of my fellow Maryknollers told me they saw a problem. I'd identified so much with my work that if my superiors were to transfer me to another mission some day, in some other part of the world, they were afraid I wouldn't obey. I asked them how they could suspect this, because I'd never even thought of being disobedient. And they said, 'Because you like your work too much. It's too much a part of you.'

"Well, the day came when their theory was put to the test. My father general wrote me a letter in which he said he intended to put me in other work in the congregation, and I should return to New York. And when I got back to the United States he asked me to take over the Maryknoll Department of Social Communications. This department is extremely important in our congregation, and it looked like too big a responsibility for me, so I said to the general, 'Fine, I'll do it. But please forget the Maryknoll custom.' The 'Maryknoll custom' is that when you are assigned anywhere it's just for a period of three years at first, to see if you should stay there or be changed. I told father general that if he saw I wasn't doing well, he should change me after three months, or six months. The only thing I was interested in, I said, was doing a really useful job. He assured me he'd do it this way. But I was reappointed three times, and I left this work only when I was finally involved full-time in my people's liberation struggle.

"All during this period, Maryknoll was expanding my horizons. I had to travel all over the missions. So I got acquainted with other experiments like the one I'd been so intensely involved with in Chile."

> *"One day, the understanding and experience of the cross suddenly became the main thing in my life."*

"Lent 1975 marked a new step in my life. It was the eve of Ash Wednesday. I was in my little office in New York. Everybody had gone home for the day. I was alone with my thoughts then, and I was wondering what I was going to do for Lent that year. How was I going to try to overcome myself and come nearer to our Lord? What was I going to ask God for, and what resolutions should I make?

"I reflected on this for some time. And I ended with a prayer. It was a simple, spontaneous, short prayer, but since that night it has never left me. 'Lord,' I prayed, 'help me understand the mystery of your cross. Help me love your cross. Give me the strength I need to accept and embrace it always.'

"And a new stage of my life began. That prayer came back to me again and again. It became a habit for me to think it, to say it. Never before had I been as faithful in carrying out my 'Lenten resolutions' as I was that Lent, as this prayer kept

welling up within me more insistently and vividly. No prayer I've
ever said has been more fruitful for my life or given me such
clear ideas, such awareness. It lighted up for me a whole series of
thoughts about what the cross really is. And it's led to a
deepening of my understanding of the mystery of the cross, and
what it means to commit yourself to live the Lord's cross.

"Here I should say that the person who had the most impact
on my life at that time, by his way of living his Christianity, was
Martin Luther King, Jr. I carried a little picture of him with me.
There were photos of him on the walls of my room. I looked at
Martin Luther King as a very special human being—someone
very consistent. I'd taken steps to get him to visit Chile before I
came back to the United States, and he'd accepted, but he didn't
make it. He was killed. I always thought of Martin Luther King
as a kind of reproach to myself, because I was so afraid to
follow in his footsteps. I looked on him as a guide, as a
standard. And yet at the same time I tried to excuse my
mediocrity by saying that he was one of those special persons,
persons whom God had made different—not me, I was afraid.
Then one day I came to the conviction that this wasn't really the
way it was. No, we were all equal—and by the grace of God we
could overcome any situation, any fear.

"Reflections such as these had led me to the prayer: 'Lord,
help me understand the mystery of your cross. Help me love
your cross. Give me the strength I need to accept and embrace it
always.' This was the beginning of the stage in my spiritual life
in which the cross, and reflection on the cross, became the main
thing for me. Before, the cross was something I felt sad about.
And logically, if you think about it enough, what you're going
to do is cry. But all of a sudden it changed into something
different. The cross transformed itself into a cradle. One symbol
of the cross is the lily—the Easter flower. I entered into a
dialectical process in which cross and resurrection are altogether
inseparable. Cross *is* resurrection.

"In this process I came to the conviction that the cross is not
just some type of suffering or other, as we so often think. If I
have an ingrown toenail, I have a cross. Anything we don't like
we call a cross. If we're suffering the consequences of our own

carelessness and faults we say that it's 'our cross,' and that we 'have to accept our cross.' But that's not the cross. The cross is the inevitable consequence of accepting the will of the Father. It's the inevitable consequence of preaching the fatherhood of God and a communion of sisters and brothers among all human beings, and denouncing everything that keeps this communion from becoming reality. When you do this—and therefore want to identify with those who hunger and thirst for justice, identify with the exploited and marginalized—you invite reprisals. When you identify with those who suffer, you take the risk of reprisals. *This* is the cross.

"Now the catch is, where there's no cross there's no Christianity. Christ wasn't crucified because he was careless, or because he lived in particularly evil times. All this hit me at once. And I started to have a brand-new understanding of what death is. What we always used to say, and meditate on—those words of our Lord, 'Greater love than this no one has, than to lay down one's life for one's brothers and sisters'—this now became something utterly real for me. I came to see that the cross was the greatest act of love. It was the total gift of love: you not only give your goods, you give your life itself. And if it's the greatest act of love, then it's the greatest act of life—it's the act where life is the most manifest. Therefore the cross is life. And here my meditation begins to consider that life can't be measured in the number of days an existence lasts, but by the depth of a commitment.

"I remember, during the liberation struggle, others would tell me I evidently was not afraid of death, in view of the fact that I got involved in something like that. 'I don't want to die,' I told them. 'I want to live—and I fear the walking death of not getting involved, and keeping silent.' To me this was mediocre existence. It turned you into a walking corpse that contaminated and corrupted everything around with its mediocrity.

"This thirst for life, for resurrection to life, is what liberates you from what most keeps you from being alive. Liberation, for me, is concentrated in an interior liberation from the chains of terror—from fear of the consequences of doing what I know I ought to do but don't do out of fear, fear of the consequences, fear of reprisals: fear of the cross. These chains have to be broken. 'Lord, help me understand, help me love, help me embrace your cross. . . .' "

> *"If I refused to help my wounded people for fear that Maryknoll might expel me, how would I explain that to our Lord?"*

"All this was to be a preparation that I didn't even imagine. It helped prepare me for the call to join my people's struggle. When I received the invitation to join, in 1976, I immediately wondered, 'What's going to happen when the church realizes? What's going to happen when Maryknoll realizes? What's the Vatican going to say?' All this passed through my mind.

"I confess that the question, 'What's going to happen when Maryknoll realizes what I'm doing?,' caused me great anxiety. I love Maryknoll and my fellow Maryknollers very much. I've always loved them. They're my family. And I thought, 'There's no way they're going to understand. They're not in my situation. There's no way I'm not going to cause them problems. They're going to have to throw me out.' And it really hurt a lot to think that this could happen. And I couldn't blame them if it did. But it really hurt, and kept hurting.

"Then I thought: 'What will Rome's reaction be?' Well, I didn't worry about this as much. It wasn't the same thing. 'They'll have to react,' I thought—'but I don't know how.' And I didn't worry much about it, because, right after, I could see myself with our Lord. 'How shall I explain it to our Lord if I don't do it?' How was I going to explain to the Lord that I was going down from Jerusalem to Jericho, and I saw my people lying all bloody in a ditch, crying for my help repeatedly, and I passed by? For fear of what for me was the worst thing that could happen to me—that Maryknoll would throw me out—I wouldn't help my wounded people? And here came my prayer again: 'Help me understand, love, and embrace the cross.'

"And so I said yes. I couldn't refuse. Not to do it would be to be a traitor to what Christ demanded of me. What was demanded of every human being was demanded much more of me, as a Christian, and as a priest.''

> *"Taking part in my people's struggle was for me a most profound religious experience."*

"What was asked of me in this struggle was something altogether compatible and consistent with my vocation. I was to make known what Nicaraguans were going through, why they were struggling, and why they had considered themselves obliged to take up armed struggle—because there was no other way out of the armed violence of the repressive Somoza dictatorship.

"My initial mission was twofold. My comrades told me, 'Miguel, we're getting ready for an insurrection, and then the revolution. We want to create a new, democratic society of brothers and sisters.' You could have knocked me over with a feather! My fellow freedom fighters had exactly the same concept of what Nicaragua was crying for as I did. They knew the work I was already doing. And now they were asking me to work in their international mission and to help form a new government. All this seemed to me to be a service that was completely consistent with the duties of anyone who, besides being a Nicaraguan, pursued a mission that included being a builder of peace—which requires that one also build justice, because there's no peace without justice—and building justice included defusing the time bomb of a situation of chronic, deep injustice afflicting our people and capable of exploding at any moment.

"Taking part in this struggle was a most profound religious experience for me. To work every day side by side with persons who were ready to give their lives in battle for their brothers and sisters—only God knows how much that converts us, draws us close to our Lord, to his cross, to his resurrection. I have never celebrated the Eucharist more meaningfully than when I celebrated it with my fellow freedom fighters. When we said,

'This is my body . . . this is my blood,' we weren't just repeating these words from a position of neutrality, from the unlikelihood that we ourselves might have to suffer. We were making Christ's words our own. We were entering into his passion really. We were entering into his cross. Besides meaning *his* body, the words 'my body' meant my own body, too, which was also prepared to be sacrificed, and 'my blood' also meant my own blood, which was ready to be poured out, shed. There, right down inside me, I discovered an authentic disposition to live what the Eucharist signifies.

"You see—how shall I put it . . .? For me the whole war was a great Eucharist, because, in all my comrades there was this disposition to give all, to give their lives. It wasn't just one person ready to give up his or her life for all the others. Every one of us had to be ready for death. Every one of us knew that death could come at any moment.

"I didn't die. But I could have died. I was that close, many a time. Right there beside you, one was taken, and one wasn't taken, and you didn't know why. I remember, when we were in hiding, every morning, when Sergio Ramírez and I went out into the street, Sergio would say, 'Well, we'll probably get it today.' And at night, before we turned out the light, Sergio would read from the Bible, and then we'd talk about what he'd read, always to draw strength from it for our commitment.

"As this period drew to a close, just before victory, it helped a lot to remember my papa's last words to me before he died. Something very unpleasant had happened. Somoza's National Guard had come looking for me. They had planted a bomb in the house, blown up my papa's office, and then come back, thirty-six of them, all armed. Then they'd headed for Sergio's house and done the same. I wasn't there. My papa was greatly concerned, and he thought I would be too, so he found out where I was and phoned me. I remember what he told me. He said, 'Look, I've talked things over with your mother, and we wanted to tell you not to worry about us. Nothing's going to happen to us.' I knew from his tone what he meant. He meant, in life or death. He meant, they can kill our body, but they can't kill *us*. 'They can't do anything to us,' he repeated, 'and I want you to know that I'm saying an extra rosary with your mother.'

They'd been praying all day. The 'extra' rosary would be number six.

" '. . . an extra rosary for you to be strong. Don't be afraid of death. And we've asked the Lord to give you the Christian "courage" (only he didn't say "courage," he used a colloquial word for gonads) to follow Christ right to Calvary if you have to, if that's his will.' This is just the way papa said it. And he added, 'The people can't be disappointed and cheated again. The people have great hopes in you, in all of you. And the only thing that would kill me is if you'd turn back *because* you were afraid to die.' "

> *"I have **to do this—out of fidelity to Christ and love for my people. The two together make up a single cross.**"*

"Something that's been very important to me is meditation on the meaning of the parable of the good Samaritan. It seems to me that we're all 'going down from Jerusalem to Jericho' in our lives, and that we're carrying with us the plans we've made, our projects and programs for the work we want to do. I had my 'responsibility,' my agenda. My life was very closely programed. I had to travel all the time, all over the world. I had my program, my schedule, all planned out a year in advance, with the exact dates and places where I had to be. But suddenly I saw my fellow Nicaraguans lying in a pool of blood and calling out to me. They were in need of help. They were in a crucial stage of their quest for conditions more in conformity with the dignity of human beings created in the image and likeness of God. And I could have said, 'Look, I have a lot of work to do, I have to keep moving—my work is very important.' I could have said 'Include me out.'

"The will of God is manifested not only in the will of superiors who live and govern on the margin of history. The will of God appears in relationship with history: it arises out of history itself. Many times it leaps out onto our path just when we're on our way to carry out our scheduled work, our programs. God leaps out onto our path with unforeseeable

things, things that take us by surprise—especially our wounded
neighbor, God's wounded people, God's and ours. Suddenly,
then, I found myself having to dismount, and attend to my
people, wounded to the death, and leave the beaten path of my
usual missionary activity. I had to follow the example, not of the
priest, but of the good Samaritan.

"I *have* to do this, out of fidelity to Christ and love for my
people—which aren't different things. They're one thing—one
faith, one love, one cross."

*"Miguel, how did your superiors and your congregation react
when they knew you were taking part in the people's struggle?"*

"Even before October 1977, when we were getting ready for
the offensive that would unleash a two-year war of liberation,
father general and the members of the General Council of
Maryknoll had noticed something 'different' about me. I
remember how one of the fathers of the General Council ran
into me one day in the corridor and asked me to step into his
room for a minute. He closed the door, and said to me, 'Look,
Miguel, we're worried about you. You seem different recently.
You seem to be going around with a tremendous load on your
shoulders. We think you've got a problem, and we were talking
about it with father general in the council. We think something's
going on. We want you to know we love you. We want you to
know that this is your family, and that we're always ready to
listen to you if something's happening to you. Something's
bothering you. You walk down the corridor now as if you
weren't yourself. You're distracted or something.'

"I'd always been very jovial, attentive to everyone. And now I
was pensive, preoccupied—especially as October drew near. I
told him no, I didn't have any problems. They shouldn't worry;
maybe it was from my sinus infection. 'Your sinusitis? A likely
story,' he said.

"When they finally found out what it was, they raised Cain.
They said I hadn't trusted them enough to tell them what was
bothering me. They'd always treated me with love, they said,
treated me as a brother. Why hadn't I been able to confide in
them? They'd have understood me, they said; they'd have

supported me, and I wouldn't have had to go around so
burdened. Well, all I could tell them was that I couldn't tell them
at that time. It was too delicate a matter.''

> *"I have the support of my
> congregation and my bishop.
> But I suffer from the fact that
> Nicaraguans have to suffer
> reprisals just because they
> want to create a more just,
> more Christian life."*

"I've always received, and still receive, tremendous
understanding from Maryknoll. Maryknoll has been a solid
pillar of support and help, a buttress, a mainstay. Maryknollers
have never let me down. They understood that this was
something unusual, but they judged me according to what had
been my attitude before—the way I always followed orders, was
always ready to do God's will. And they understand that right
now I see that this is the will of God for me and there's no way
out of it. They're on the journey with me, in prayer. In their
Eucharist they always pray that I may never betray my
conscience. The only thing I can say about Maryknoll is that I'm
grateful and thankful for the generosity and understanding that
my congregation and my superiors have shown me.

"My superiors have assigned me to the diocese of Estelí now.
And here too I find nothing but generous understanding and
support on the part of Bishop Rubén López. I feel very close to
him and his pastoral team—the priests, the nuns, and the lay
ministers.

"I try to be with them as much as I can, not only on retreats or
days of recollection, but in the other pastoral meetings held in
the diocese. I'd like to be able to participate a lot more. But I
keep in contact with my bishop. It's true I travel a great deal, but
I see him whenever I come back from a long trip. So we get
together often. This has been a source of energy and grace for
me and has kept the cross from being even heavier.

"The cross is very heavy just now. All this hostile activity, all this aggressiveness on the part of the world's most reactionary currents—the United States and other national and regional groupings united in the cause of aggression against Nicaragua —all this is part of the cross we have to suffer, not just I, but all our companions in the revolution, and the whole people of Nicaragua, who suffer reprisals for trying to create a more just life situation, a more Christian community of brothers and sisters.

"When I saw this I really had to say to myself that it was a fine state of affairs! Never before had I seen a situation where a whole country so clearly needed the church to try to influence the hearts of its members and incline them toward the gospel, so that the people would be equal to the demands of this unique stage in its history. What Nicaraguans are trying to do, of course, is create a genuine society of sisters and brothers. And I kept thinking: the atmosphere is right, the soil is right, we've got this determination to make our revolution succeed—but we always have to fight selfishness, and this is the essential moral ministry of the church, its basic ethical task.

"The church should get into it the way Christopher Mwoleka did. He's the bishop of Rulengue, in Tanzania. I greatly love and admire that man—the way he talked about the role of the church in a revolution, where structures are changing to permit the practice—not just the theory—of a more brotherly and sisterly life together, a society of justice for all. This bishop explained what the church should do in such a case: work to lift hearts, widen hearts, unburden them, so that Christians would be able to throw themselves wholeheartedly into their task in the spirit of the gospel. This is what I was hoping for here. But I haven't seen it.

"What I've seen here is that the attitude of some of the members of our church has done a great deal of harm to the church, and to the church's image. But our church survives in spite of us, because God is God. The worst enemies of the church were never outside it. We ourselves are its worst enemies, because of our inconsistency. We're the ones, when we command subjugated peoples to give up their struggle for independence and liberation. We're the ones, when we support oppressive regimes and bless the armies that set forth to persecute and kill patriots. And all this in the name of Christ! Here's where the problem is.

"What I've seen here strengthens my conviction that many have turned away from the church, not to part company with Christ, but to separate themselves from a church that has itself turned away from God by turning its back on the poor."

> *"There's a certain very painful lack of comprehension. It makes me afraid they want me to leave the priesthood."*

"What has made the cross much heavier for me is the lack of understanding on the part of some of the members of the church, some priests, and even some members of the hierarchy. My experience had always been very positive as to relationships with my superiors and the hierarchy. Always. And when difficulties, problems, or differences of opinion came up, it had always been my experience that they were solved in dialogue— human, evangelical, ecclesial dialogue. And never once—until I came here to Nicaragua—never once did I have the experience of a closed-minded authority, an authority saying this is the way it is to be 'because I say so.' I'd never had this experience. And so, when I was transferred here, my first two years were years of tremendous anguish. Sometimes I'd think 'I'm going to go crazy here!' I actually felt the physical pain of anguish. I felt physical pressure, as if there were some huge, unbearable rock pressing down on my chest.

"Having to watch this whole closing off of a part of the church—which, besides not positively evangelizing, saw everything negatively, saw only faults in others, never in itself—having to see all this has caused me great pain, has hurt me deeply. Never before, in all my priestly life, have I ever thought, even for a second, that I could leave the priesthood. But here, at certain moments, when I have to face this very painful lack of comprehension, I've had to think that maybe they're trying to get me to leave the priesthood. And when I

think of the possibility of expulsion, or excommunication, or
suspension, sometimes the thought has flashed through my
mind: 'Well, if I'm being rejected like this, why don't I just go
get a girl friend?' The thought doesn't last longer than a couple
of seconds, and it's very rare, because, after all, I've given that
up forever. I have a commitment, and I intend to be faithful to
it to the day I die. But I have to admit to you that this has
happened to me here, for the first time in my life—and not by
any desire of mine, but by reason of all this pressure and lack of
understanding.

"But now I'm no longer so shocked and surprised. God has
given me the grace to accept this attitude, in certain ecclesiastical
persons, as being a reaction that, far from being unusual, tends
to be typical—historically typical, whenever Christian peoples
have been struggling in crucial moments in their history, striving
to build a more worthy and more just society. I've had to accept
this as a fact, a regrettable fact, in the hope that, despite all, the
human race may forge ahead. There's an irreversible process
afoot in history, and you can't hold it back. And it's not a
process that goes against the faith or against God. Quite the
contrary, it's a historical process that, however much it may take
some church members by surprise, so that they don't see God in
it, God is bringing forward. It's a step toward his kingdom of
justice and peace."

> *"I'm not a completely happy
> person, but I do have great
> peace. To have been delivered
> from the fear of reprisals has
> made me free in the face of
> death."*

*"In the midst of all this, Miguel, how is your spirit—your faith,
your peace? Do you feel 'fulfilled,' or are you frustrated?"*

"I can't say I'm a completely happy person. I do feel very
fulfilled, but there's always been sorrow in my life. It's the same
sadness I felt when I was a little boy, when I saw all the

inequalities and injustice here in Nicaragua. That pain is still there. It's as if there were a wound in my heart and somebody suddenly pours vinegar onto it.

"But this pain doesn't take away my peace. I have great peace. I have a certitude, a great hope. I never have problems of conscience. I used to. I used to be ashamed of myself. I felt there was something I was supposed to do, but I wasn't entirely willing to do it, because I was afraid of reprisals. To have been delivered from these chains and bonds of fear, this fear of reprisals—this has made me feel really free. It has placed me in a state of permanent readiness to die. I know that we're a target, and that we can be killed at any moment. My fellow revolutionaries sometimes tell me I'm not taking sufficient security measures. I don't know, I might be irresponsible here, but it isn't something that bothers me. For a long time now I've been ready and willing to be an instrument of the Lord for however long he may wish. Death is not an enemy I fear. It doesn't frighten me.

"In fact, sometimes I feel very weary, and I say, 'Oh, my Lord, now's the time. Call me now.' Sometimes I just really feel tired, tired, so tired. But I get my energy back and keep forging ahead. How long yet? Well, I don't know. God knows.''

> ***"When I heard we couldn't
> say Mass, I cried all night."***

"How did you feel, Miguel, when, in July 1981, you had to give up celebrating Mass and all other priestly functions?"

"Remember I told you that the only thing my papa ever told me to do in all my life was when I was alone there in California. He told me to go to daily Mass and say the rosary, our Lady's rosary. I remember papa used to tell us that the Mass was the most important thing there was. Once I asked him why he thought it was so important. And he said, 'Because the most important thing in life is to please God, and nothing pleases God more than the sacrifice of his Son, which we commemorate at Mass.'

"For a long time this explanation, just this, was enough for me. It was a matter of pleasing God, and the Mass is the thing that pleases God the most. So you had to go to Mass.

"Then I immersed myself in my theological studies. And Jungmann's *The Canon of the Mass* helped me understand my father's explanation better. The Mass became the center of my life. And the two things I always liked best to preach on, in every sort of retreat or sermon I had to give, was the Mass and the Holy Trinity. I looked on all of life as a preparation for the next Mass, and the fulfillment of the commitment made in the last Mass. This is what Vatican II said—the whole Christian life, the whole life of the church, and especially the life of a priest, springs from the Mass and culminates in the Mass. The Eucharist is our life's spring and source, its pinnacle and crown. And even if I'd never said but one Mass in my life, that Mass would have been the high point of my life, because of what I had celebrated, lived, and committed in that one Mass.

"Daily Mass was always my greatest joy. I've never been a parish priest. In Maryknoll I got in the habit of concelebrating with my co-workers, in a little chapel we'd set up on the top floor of the building where we had our Department of Social Communications. Before that, I used to say Mass in a convent every day, for the sisters there. That was a very nice time. I loved to celebrate Mass with persons I knew were totally committed.

"During the war in Nicaragua, I've already told you my experience. That was when my celebrations of the Eucharist were best, with persons ready to give everything—their body, their blood, their whole life.

"And so, when the agreement was made with the bishops of Nicaragua whereby we priests in government were no longer to celebrate Mass, not even privately, it was the hardest, most painful blow I have ever had to suffer in my life. The day the decision came I was out of the country. Father Fernando Cardenal phoned me in Mexico City. I remember, and I'm not ashamed to tell you, I cried all night that night. I couldn't sleep, and I cried and I cried into my pillow. It hurt terribly.

"But what hurt the most was that it seemed to me that it would be very harmful to the church. Because, really, it was too much. It looked almost like meanness, like punishment—for something I'd never considered a crime. It seemed to me that this punishment would hurt the church's image and thus hurt the people. The church is, of course, very important for the people, as long as it's faithful, as long as the salt keeps its savor.

"It hurt very, very much to be deprived of celebrating Mass. And I have to confess that I haven't always been faithful to the agreement. Sometimes when I travel and meet fellow Maryknollers, I celebrate Mass with them. I've even celebrated in the Maryknoll headquarters chapel, on instructions from father general. He told me not to be afraid. And I've done it in the Estelí cathedral, concelebrating with my bishop. But I do try not to cause problems with the hierarchy. Here, in this house, which I built partly with Mass in mind, we did celebrate Mass before; I have a portable altar in my room, and government personnel came here to Mass. But here I absolutely don't do it now, so I won't seem to be looking for trouble.

"I used to have Mass here all the time, and persons came here who didn't go to church, even some army officers who told me they didn't go to church because there were some—even a bishop—who said they went to church only to be seen. So they came here so as not to be seen."

> *"I don't feel like an unshatterable rock. The strongest temptations I've had are temptations not to forgive someone."*

"Not to be able to say Mass was a heavy blow. But the Lord knows how to make up for it. Christ is very much alive and very real for me in my neighbor, in the people. I love him in loving my people. I serve him in serving my people, in struggling for peace, struggling for worthy, respectful relationships with other countries and governments. And I have my faith in the Lord. And I feel stronger and stronger as this faith broadens to include faith in other human beings and their history.

"And I think there's nothing that can tear us away from the Lord. Nothing can separate us from our Lord—only we ourselves. It can't come from outside, it can only come from within.

"I do believe I'm in a touchy situation. We're all weak, and temptations can come very suddenly. The greatest temptations I've felt, it seems to me, are not to want to forgive right away.

And the Mass is the most important thing where forgiveness is concerned. At Mass, if you have something against your brother or sister, you're supposed to leave your gift at the altar and go and pardon your sister or brother and then come back and pray the Mass. And so now that I can't say Mass any more, I ask the Lord to supply for this, to make up for this, so that there will be no trace of anything like a lack of love and understanding and forgiveness.

"It's not an ideal situation. It's a painful situation, and I'd say it's even a dangerous one. But here is where we keep praying, asking the Lord to help us to be faithful even without our normal supports, the ones that God had always granted us before, to hold us up.

"And I want to say that my meetings with my bishop and the whole pastoral team of Estelí—meetings I wish were much more frequent, if I only had the time—are tremendously rich for me. Really, for me, Estelí is a wellspring of life and vitality. I don't know if this sort of thing has been there all the time, or if our Lord is making me see more of it now. Anyway, I certainly see it now, and I feel tremendously strengthened and confirmed in my faith when, besides my private prayer, which is constant in my life, I have the opportunity to devote some time to these meetings, and leave aside the other tasks and duties that are absorbing me at the moment and forget about them. When I do have this time to devote solely and exclusively to Christian and priestly community reflection, I notice a great enrichment, and this effect lasts a long time. I don't know what would have become of my faith if I hadn't had this support. God knows. I don't. Maybe the problem would have been solved in some other way.

"But even after all these years in the priestly life, I have to confess I'm weak. I don't feel like an unshatterable rock. I feel greatly in need of support. There's no way around it: the faith has been dealt a blow. But my faith is strengthened by the support I receive from Maryknoll, from the diocese I'm assigned to but don't live in, and by so much I see of God in the patience, the goodness, the sacrifice, and the readiness to forgive, of the persons I work with, share with, and converse with so frankly— Daniel, Sergio, Humberto, Norita, Bayardo, and the others. My faith grows stronger especially when I see priests who take a position consistent with their priesthood, and know that they'll have to suffer the consequences of that position. All this strengthens my faith.

"But in spite of all this I'm weak. I have to admit I'm hard hit by an attitude that, to my view, is antipatriotic—an attitude not of solidarity with the interests of the people, but with the interests of the class that's always held the privileges in our society. This inconsistent attitude, this attitude of profound fear of history, and of overconcern on the part of the church for itself instead of for the people, is a real blow.

"I believe that what should be more important to the church than anything else is a concern for the people, for whom our Lord became incarnate, lived, suffered, died, and rose again. This is the church's raison d'être, its mission. The church should not be obsessed with the 'rights of the church,' but with the rights of the people. I don't think the church has any rights above and beyond the rights of all the sons and daughters of God—which are most sacred rights, and ought to be respected and defended in everyone's behalf.

"I don't think the church needs to go looking for privileges and extraordinary rights in order to accomplish its mission. Its mission is not to be concerned for itself, but to be consistent with the faith—not to live so concerned about what will happen tomorrow, but to be concerned with what we are doing today: what we are, and what we are doing; not what will happen to us. When I see all this preoccupation with the 'rights of the church,' and I realize that this is how the illegitimate interests of certain sectors of society are defended, my faith is dealt a blow, and weakened."

"I've never been concerned to defend myself. What I worry about is that the people are misunderstood—that others want to condemn the people unjustly."

"You're surely aware of the objections and accusations made against you and your fellow priests in government in certain circles: ambition, love of power, partisanship, disobedience,

treachery. . . . Has any of these accusations made a particular impression on you? Would you like to answer them?"

"Teófilo, I think the thing that's always made the least impression on me, and that least worries me now, is blame and misunderstanding directed toward me or what I do. I don't mean I'm not interested in knowing what the criticisms are.

"One of the things that has stuck with me best from my novitiate days is the importance of listening to criticism. The novice master used to insist on it. He used to say it was too bad that friends criticize one another only when they're annoyed, and that others who generally criticize us don't care whether, they hurt us or not and so they come out with just anything. I've always thought it important to listen to criticism. But I don't feel hurt and I don't need to defend myself. I'm not afraid, I don't get obsessed. I consider that the one I'll really have to answer to is our Lord, and yes, this does interest me. I'm interested in being able to justify, to the Lord, what I've done, and what I haven't done—what I've failed to do.

"What concerns me right now is not a misunderstanding of me, but a misunderstanding of my people. This people, by all the means at its disposal, is seeking to overcome a situation that, from the Christian viewpoint, as from the human viewpoint, is intolerable and unacceptable. And there are those who want to condemn the people. I'm concerned that they want to condemn those who, for the first time in the history of Nicaragua, battle to the death to create a genuinely just, genuinely worthy society—with all the errors they've committed, and keep on committing, because it's we humans who make revolutions, and we humans make mistakes.

"To see that there's something so deep here, something so worthy of being understood and supported by Christians, and then to see counter-revolutionary positions crop up that coincide with, and become manipulated by, the known intentions and actions of North American imperialism, and to see part of the church assuming these antipopular attitudes—that hurts and concerns me. Respect for my person has never been one of my worries, and I've never made any effort to defend myself, because I'm not trying to be approved and applauded, or elected to anything; the only thing I'm trying to do is be authentic."

"What do I hope for? To be able to embrace the cross, in whatever form it comes."

"Miguel, what are your feelings about, or your attitude to, the possibility that priests might be ordered to leave their government posts?"

"As a human being, as a Nicaraguan, as a Christian, and as a priest, I have to react in view of the de facto situations in which my life places me. In my opinion, there is no real contradiction between my priestly ministry and my complementary ministries in service to the people—though in the mind of someone else, who might happen to be my superior at the moment, such a contradiction might seem to exist. But I'm always going to be obedient.

"On the other hand, I'll never betray my conscience out of false obedience. And I have a clear awareness that loyalty to the people, especially to the most oppressed and marginalized and historically exploited of my people, has to be the concrete form my fidelity to Christ will take.

"I don't think there's any doubt, then, what my response would be in case I were called on to do something that I'd consider a betrayal of the people. My response will be (and God grant that it may be this): to be able to embrace the cross in whatever form I'm asked to accept it."

•

Miguel downed the last mouthful of his lemonade. ("Sinusitis dehydrates me.") He had changed position in his hammock a number of times, and finally sat up in it, uncomfortably, concentrating on his story.

It was noon now, and I was leaving. Miguel told me he liked working in the garden. It reminded him of his noviceship, he said. He pointed out a plant that grew all around the house —low, with an abundance of thick, fleshy leaves; it was called "Holy Spirit." Another, with very pretty flowers, was "Christ's Cloak."

I walked down toward the center of Managua. Pedestrians were already calling out the "greeting of gladness." This afternoon and evening—the vigil of the Immaculate Conception—Nicaraguans say to one another, "Why this joy?" And the response is "Mary's Conception!" This is how it will be on every street, in every city, village, and hamlet in Nicaragua tonight. Tonight they will sing songs and set off rockets and pour out love—generously—sharing gifts of candy, lemons, *chicha* liquor, and sugar cane, as if there could never be an end.

Epilogue:
Confession of Faith

As a first response to the communication of the Nicaraguan
    Bishops' Conference,
we wish to say, to the bishops of Nicaragua,
        to our brother priests and the faithful of the Catholic
            Church,
        to our brothers and sisters in the faith of Christ,
        to our compatriots,
        and to all men and women of good will:

We believe in God the Father, Creator of the world and human
        beings.
We believe in Jesus Christ, the Son of God, our Brother and our
        Savior.
We believe in the church, the visible Body of Christ, to which we
        belong.
We believe in justice, the basis of human community and
        communion.
We believe in love, the first and principal commandment of
        Jesus.
We believe in our priesthood, which is our vocation to serve our
        brothers and sisters.
We believe in our country, that great family to which we belong
        and to which we owe our being.
We believe in the Nicaraguan people's revolution, fashioned by
        the people in order to overthrow tyranny and sow justice
        and love.
We believe in the poor, who will be the ones to build a more just
        homeland, and who will help us to be saved ourselves.

This is our faith and our hope—
and in accordance with these beliefs of ours, we have sought to
      serve our compatriots
in the offices in which we have been placed by them.
And we shall continue to do so, in whatsoever place
our presence and service may be necessary.

For our offices and tasks have given us:
      the power to serve, not the power to dominate,
      the power to divest ourselves of our comforts, not the
         power to enrich ourselves,
      the power to be like Christ in the service of our brothers and
         sisters,
      the power to exercise our priesthood, not to separate
         ourselves from our vocation, and
      the power to be available and open to hear and obey the
         voice of God.

In order to remain steadfast in our faith, hope, and love,
as well as in our firm resolve to serve,
we stand in need of the good will,
      the understanding,
      the counsel,
      and the prayers
of our brothers, the bishops,
      our brother priests,
      and our brothers and sisters, the laity.

Finally, we affirm our unshakable commitment to the
      Sandinista Popular Revolution,
in loyalty to our people—which is to say, in fidelity to the will of
      God.

      (Rev.) Miguel d'Escoto, (Rev.) Ernesto Cardenal
      (Rev.) Edgar Parrales, (Rev.) Fernando Cardenal

Managua, June 8, 1981,
"Year of Defense and Production"